TASTES OF THE CAMINO

30 AUTHENTIC RECIPES ALONG THE FRENCH WAY

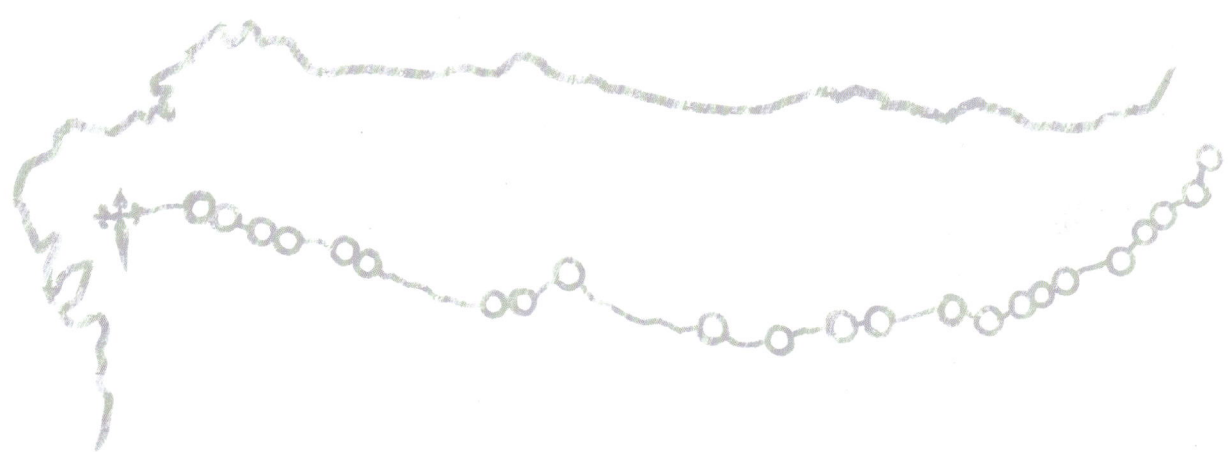

YOSMAR MONIQUE MARTÍNEZ

Copyright © 2016 Yosmar Monique Martinez

Illustrations copyright © 2016 Luis Javier Martinez
Photographs copyright © 2016 Paul L.R. Du Bois

All rights reserved. No part of this publication may be reproduced, stored in a retrieval system, or transmitted, in any form or by any means, electronic, mechanical, photocopying, recording, or otherwise, without prior written permission of the author.

Published by Whisk & Spatula, LLC
www.whiskandspatula.com
yosmar@whiskandspatula.com

Library of Congress Cataloging-in-Publication Data
Martinez, Yosmar Monique
    Tastes of the Camino: 30 Authentic Recipes along the French Way / Yosmar Monique Martinez
Includes index

ISBN: 978-0-9972534-0-5
LCCN: 2016901444

Book design: Luis Javier Martinez (@LuigiPanda)
Index: Under the Oaks Indexing

First Edition
Printed in China

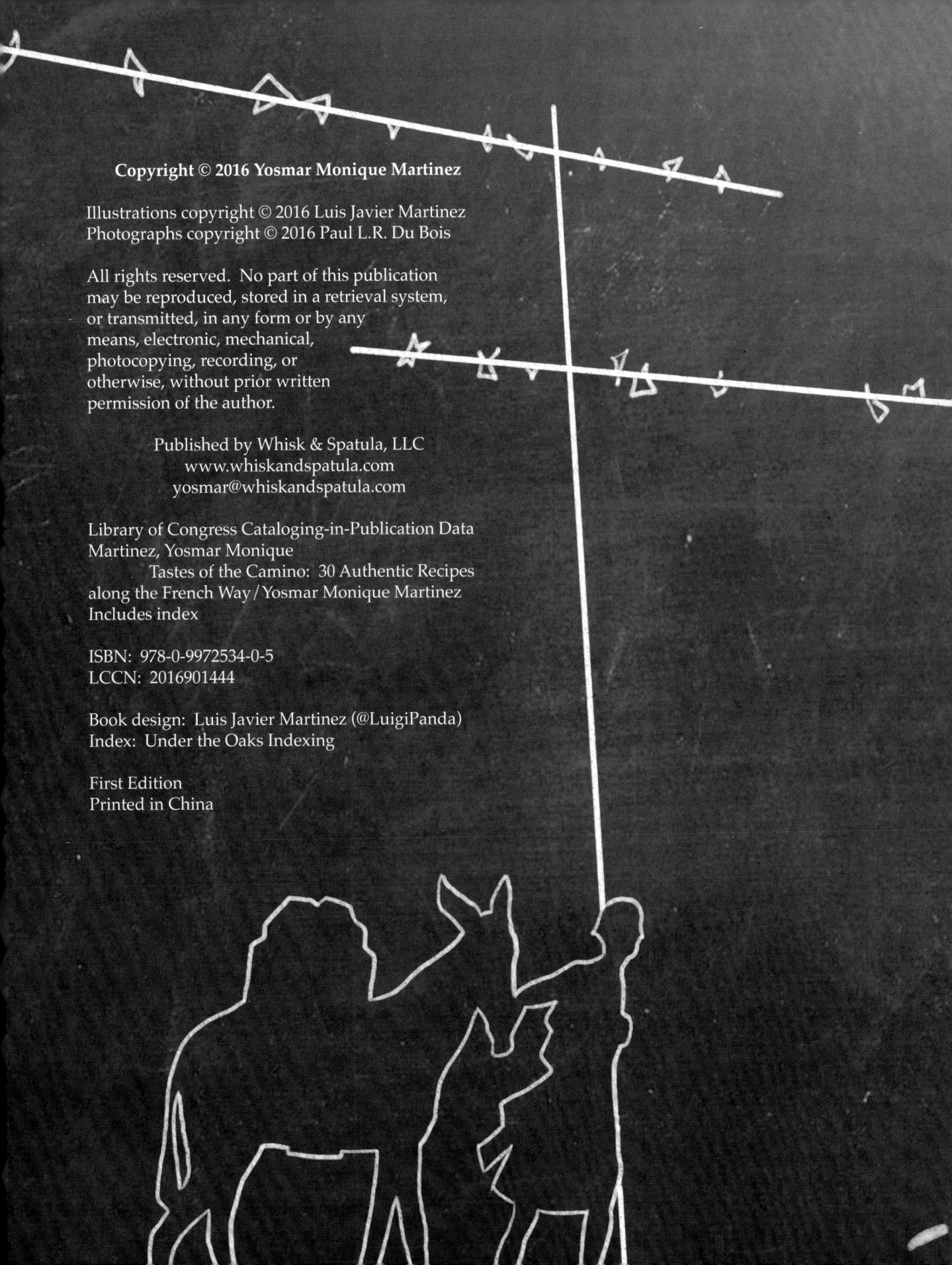

For Willie]
¡Buen Provecho!

Monin M.

DEDICATED

TO MY PARENTS, TETÉ AND ÁNGEL,

FOR ALWAYS ENCOURAGING ME TO EXPLORE THE WORLD.

TO THE "CAMINO COOKBOOK FAMILY" WHICH LIFE HAS GIVEN ME:
Thank you for all your love, insight, and encouragement!

A book does not come to life solely on the efforts of an author alone. There were many friends who volunteered to assist with the creation of this book. Without their kindness, generosity and involvement, this book would still be on my bucket list.

First of all, I must thank Janine Davis. She not only suggested I write a book but also was my sounding board and kept me focused when I lost direction in this long project.

John Rafferty made wonderful culinary introductions in Santiago that allowed me to learn the tricks that transform a good recipe into a great recipe.

Jill Silverman Hough gave me invaluable advice on how to navigate the detailed process of writing a cookbook. Her approachability and willingness to share are a true gift.

My team of recipe testers was truly a dream team! Their input was key to ensuring the quality of the recipes:
Kris Ashton, Martha Crites, Katy Dashiell, Janine Davis, Michelle Swierczynski Davis, Mariela Díaz-Butler, Laura Domínguez, Maritza Espinal, Cheryl Grasmoen, Bill Hahne, Nancy Harlan, Maryann Heidtke, Kathy Kennerly, Sara Marín de Martínez, Elaine Marshall, Carlos Mentley, Isabel Pino, John Rafferty, Luana Massi Scartezzini, Walt Scherer, Lisa Signori, Laura Simmons, Sheila Aceves, Liz Stevens, Rosa Torres-Tumazos, Isabel Valdívia, Stacey Wittig

Unbeknownst to him, Christos Costandinides planted a seed that was instrumental in my decision to walk the Camino the first time around. He also suggested a title that really captures the essence of this book.

Cheryl Grasmoen and Stephen Shields diligently proofread my book, even in the midst of family commitments and unforeseen personal circumstances.

Santiago Vitagliano provided me with my author photograph. To be able to capture someone as camera-averse as me in such a lovely manner is pure art.

There are too many pilgrims to name with whom I shared wonderful meals along the Camino. Their company and the memories of those shared meals inspired many of the recipes featured in this book.

Finally, I must thank my parents, Teté and Ángel Martínez. My mother has joined me on multiple Caminos and is always a lovely travel companion. My father has allowed me to take my mother away from him for weeks at a time and is always supportive of our passion for travel in general and the Camino in particular.

CONTENTS

INTRODUCTION - AN UNEXPECTED JOURNEY — 8

COOKING TIPS — 12

PAYS BASQUE — 15

NAVARRA — 25

LA RIOJA — 51

CASTILLA Y LEÓN — 65

GALICIA — 115

SANTIAGO — 137

INDEX — 148

AN UNEXPECTED
JOURNEY

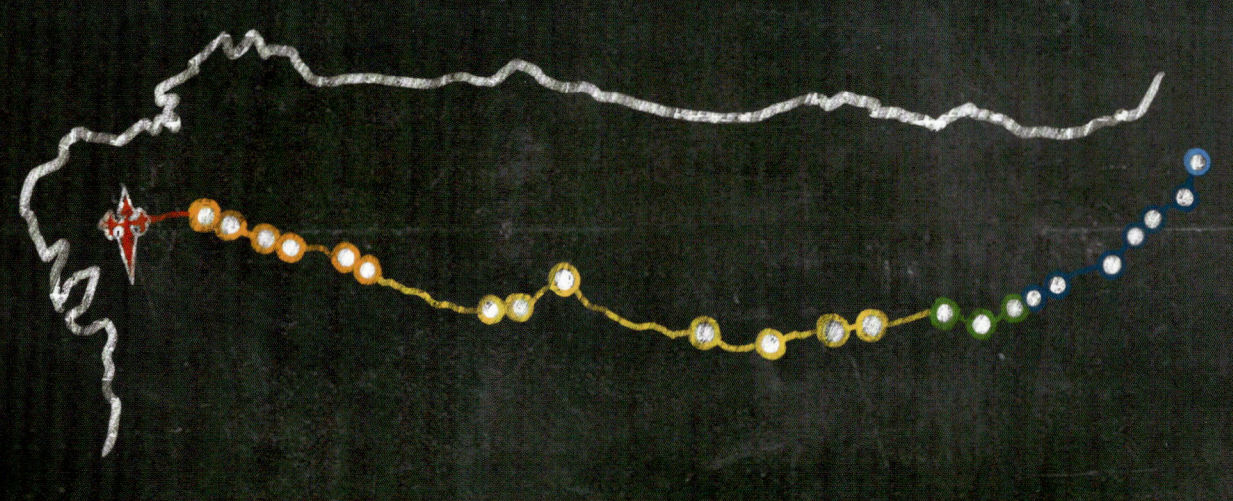

Back in 2010, my mother called me one day and asked if I knew anything about the *Camino de Santiago de Compostela* (also known as St. James's Way), a series of medieval pilgrimage routes all culminating at the Cathedral of Santiago in northwestern Spain, where the remains of the apostle St. James the Great are believed to be buried. She wondered if I would ever consider walking it to which I casually responded: "Maybe someday." She immediately informed me: "When you decide to go, let me know . . . I'm going with you." We made no concrete plans and the conversation was quickly forgotten—until a year later when I realized that I needed to get away for some much-needed time to reflect on the course of my life. I recalled our conversation and a couple of others that I had had with friends who had walked the Camino. A great curiosity about the Camino was growing in me and I realized that I was ready to go. My mother eagerly accepted my invitation to join me and we settled for a departure date only four weeks away. We scrambled to book airplane tickets, gather our bearings, and—most importantly— buy gear that we knew nothing about, neither of us being experienced hikers.

In the midst of our planning, a friend suggested I write about my Camino experience. While appealing, I knew that many personal accounts of the Camino had already been published. If I were to undertake the laborious process of writing a book, I wanted to be sure that it would be different from what already existed. So I decided to keep a daily Camino journal with the hopes that it would provide the clarity I needed to write a book. We had a wonderful Camino with all of its pains, challenges, and joys—but no book revealed itself.

A number of months later, in the middle of a ten-mile walk in Miami Beach, it occurred to me that were I on the Camino, I would be searching for breakfast number two right now. Pilgrim metabolisms tend to speed up significantly and having multiple breakfasts on any given day is as ubiquitous as the *menú de peregrino*, the inexpensive three-course menu offered to pilgrims all along the way. I realized I had to write about food on the Camino. Experiencing food—learning about, preparing, and eating it—is one of my greatest passions and when it brings loved ones together, it is joy in its purest form! In addition, I once attended culinary school at Le Cordon Bleu in Paris and enjoy sharing my knowledge of food with others.

While I have walked various Camino routes four times, the focus of this book is on foods along the Camino Francés, the most travelled route to Santiago de Compostela. Some of these foods can be found on other Camino routes (or throughout Spain), while others are pretty unique to some of the towns on the Francés. This book is laid out in the order of the regions and towns I travelled through—and where I had amazing meals—even mentioning the specific restaurant when possible. For those of you who have walked the Camino, I hope the thirty recipes in this book allow you to relive some of your Camino food experiences at home and bring back wonderful memories of meals shared with other pilgrims, an integral part of any Camino. For those of you who have yet to set foot on the Camino, perhaps these recipes will give you one more thing to look forward to while embarking on one of the most meaningful life experiences you will ever have.

¡Buen Provecho & Buen Camino!
Yosmar Monique Martinez

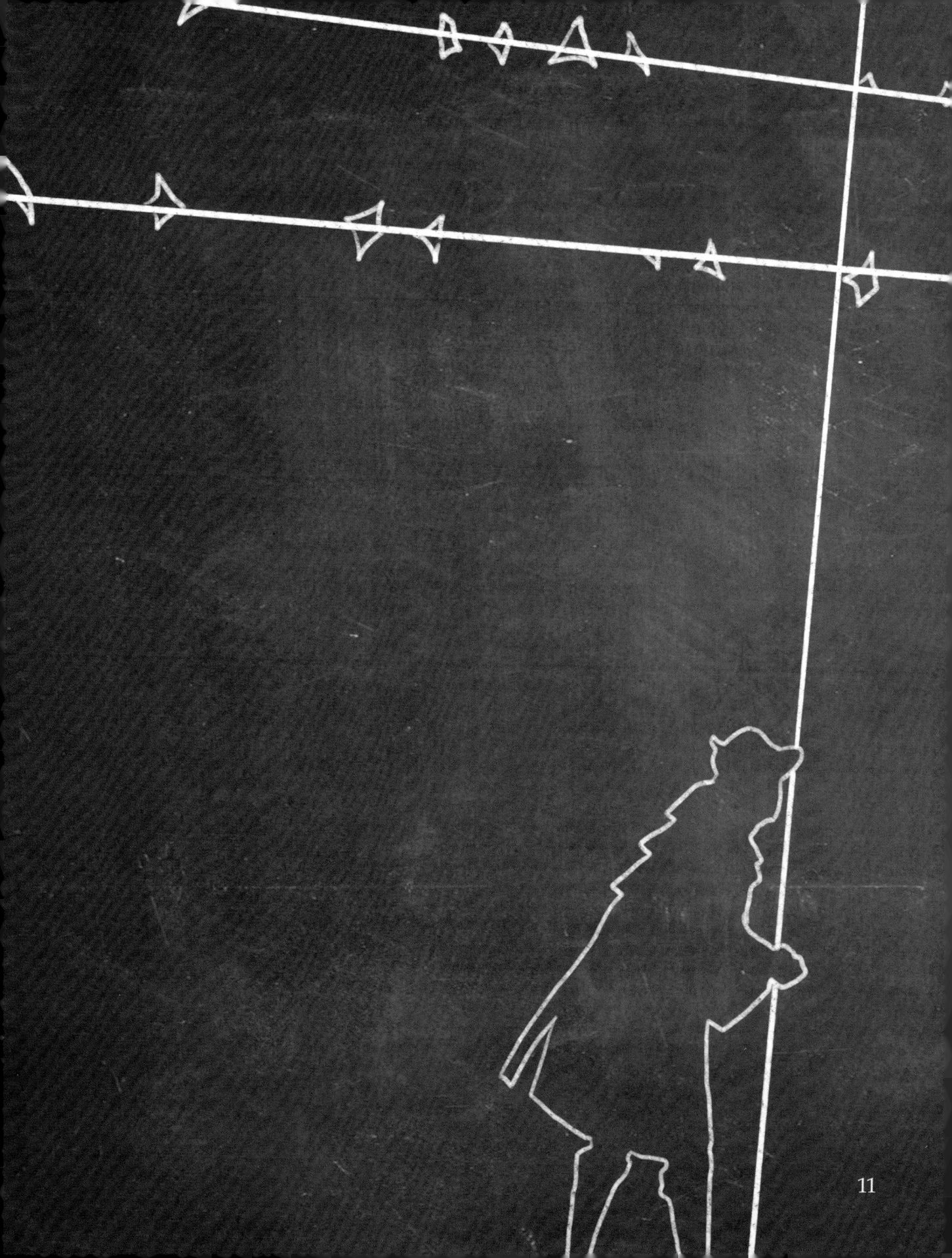

COOKING TIPS

Many people are frequently intimidated by recipes and cooking. Here are some basic cooking tips that I hope will ease your way through cooking the recipes in this book—and elsewhere.

LET'S START WITH READING THE RECIPE...

This may sound obvious but reading the *whole* recipe *before* beginning to cook is critical. By reading the recipe in full before starting to cook, you will not only know what ingredients you need and in what quantities, but you will be able to better understand the full cooking process. You will understand why a certain step must happen before another for instance, or how the ingredients must be prepped. This will, in turn, help you time your prep and cooking times, which is critical when you are having guests over for a meal. Personally, I always review my recipes one or two days beforehand. This allows me to buy whatever ingredients I don't have in stock and even do some prep work beforehand, making the actual cooking and entertaining as stress free as possible.

MISE-EN-WHAT?

The one thing I find that makes cooking really manageable is getting into the habit of always having a *mise-en-place*. "Mise-en-place" is a French culinary term that means "to put in place." Basically, it is a way to organize yourself in the kitchen. You measure out and prep all the ingredients for a recipe *before* you even begin cooking. That way, you can ensure you have all the required ingredients on hand. In addition, it helps you speed up the actual cooking process. For instance, if your onions are chopped and ready to go, when the recipe calls for them, everything will go smoothly . . . No burning of one ingredient while you are prepping another!

DIVIDED? BY HOW MUCH?

Many recipes will call for a certain amount of an ingredient "divided." For example, my recipe for *croquetas* calls for "2½ cups of flour, divided." This simply means you'll use a portion of the flour at one point in the recipe (in this example, to make the béchamel sauce) and more at another point (to bread the croquetas). It doesn't mean you should divide the total amount of flour in half, however. Hence why reading the recipe beforehand is essential to understanding how much of the ingredient (flour, in this example) goes into the recipe at each step.

SEASON TO TASTE . . . YOUR TASTE!

Whenever the recipe instructs you to "season to taste," taste the recipe before adding any salt or pepper. This will give you a baseline. Then add a bit of salt and pepper and taste again. Repeat this process until you feel the food is perfectly seasoned. Don't be afraid of salt . . . it is your friend!

SHOPPING FOR SPANISH INGREDIENTS

I find that, nowadays, assuming you live in a metropolitan area, you can find most ingredients for the recipes in this book at your regular grocery store—or at least at a local gourmet food store. However, occasionally, there are a few ingredients that I cannot find locally, and I must turn to dedicated online Spanish specialty stores such as La Tienda (www.latienda.com) or The Spanish Table (www.spanishtable.com).

TASTES OF THE CAMINO

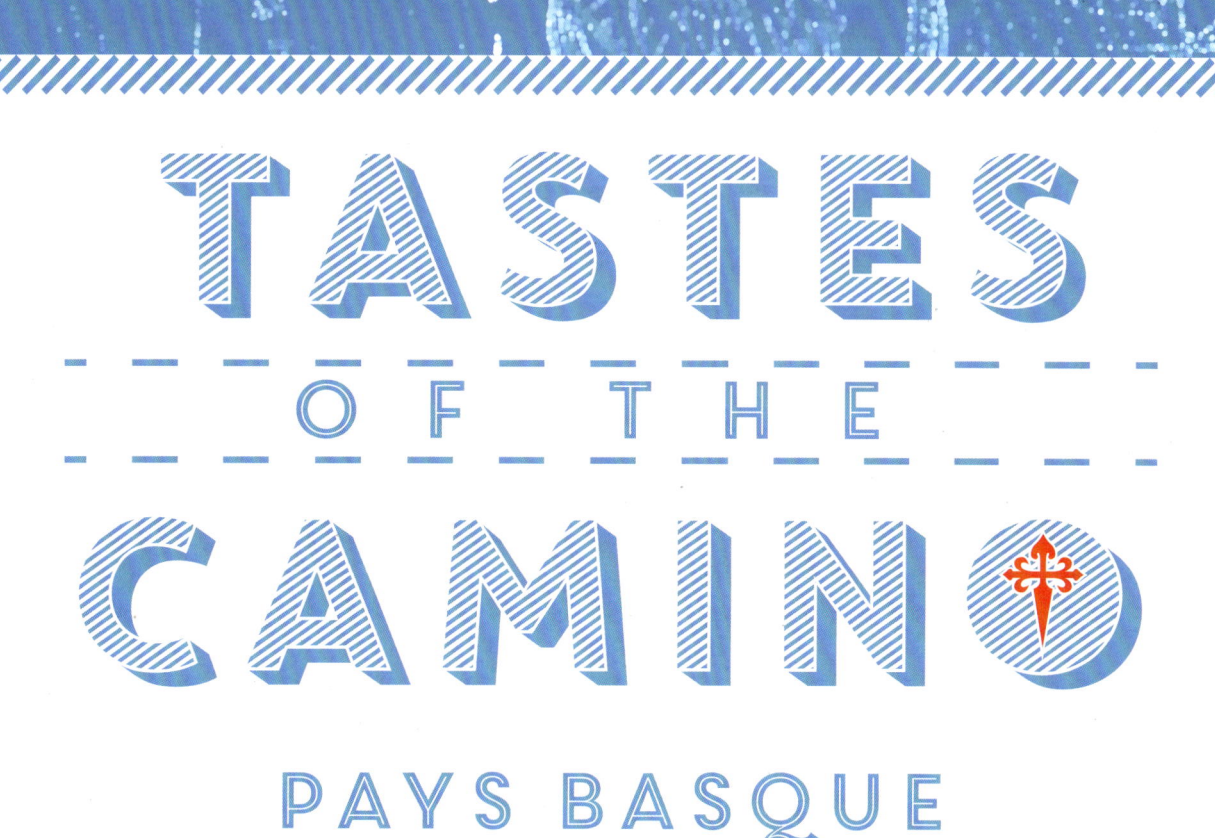

PAYS BASQUE

PAYS BASQUE

TASTES OF THE CAMINO

SAINT-JEAN-PIED-DE-PORT

POULET À LA BASQUE

Basque Chicken

I call this recipe my "Camino Baptism." It is a recipe that I learned to make many years ago while in culinary school in France. While I had not been to the French Basque country prior to my first Camino, I always loved this recipe. The chicken is always juicy, and the green and red bell pepper sauce is incredibly flavorful. Hence, when I arrived in Saint-Jean-Pied-de-Port on both of my pilgrimages along the Camino Francés, I had no doubt in my mind what I was having for dinner.

Poulet à la Basque is traditionally made with a whole chicken cut into eight parts. I prefer making it only with chicken thighs, as they tend to cook more evenly and work well with the slow-cooking method this recipe calls for.

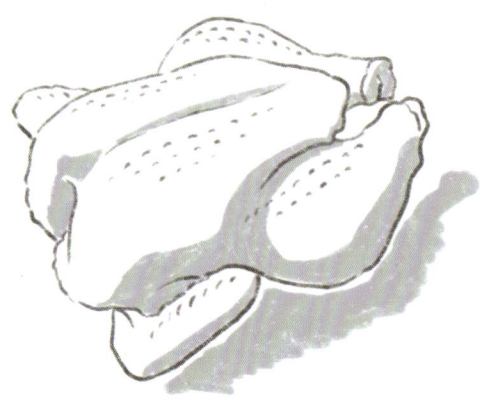

Serves 4–6

PAYS BASQUE
TASTES OF THE CAMINO

SAINT-JEAN-PIED-DE-PORT

POULET À LA BASQUE

Basque Chicken

INGREDIENTS

- 8 chicken thighs
- 2 tablespoons (30 ml) olive oil
- 1 large onion, sliced into strips
- 4 garlic cloves, minced
- 2 red bell peppers, sliced into strips
- 2 green bell peppers, sliced into strips
- 1 cup (250 ml) chopped tomatoes (approximately one 14-ounce can)
- ½ cup (120 ml) white wine
- 4 ounces (120 g) Serrano or Bayonne ham, cut into strips
- 1 tablespoon chopped flat leaf parsley (about 2 sprigs)
- 1 teaspoon (5 g) sugar (optional)
- Salt and pepper to taste

Season chicken with salt and pepper. Pour olive oil into a large sauté pan and add the chicken pieces, sautéing them on both sides until they are light golden brown. Remove chicken and set aside.

Add the onion, garlic, bell peppers, and tomatoes to the sauté pan and cook on low heat for about 10 minutes. Add the white wine and cover. Continue to cook on low for an additional 30 minutes. Season the sauce to taste with salt, pepper, and, if necessary, sugar (to cut the acidity of the tomatoes). Return the chicken to the sauté pan. Cover the pan and cook over low heat for another 20-25 minutes.

In the meantime, pan fry the ham strips in a small skillet just until slightly crisp. Once the chicken is done (when pierced, the juices should run clear), transfer the chicken and the sauce to a serving platter. Sprinkle the chicken with the crisp ham strips and parsley.

PAYS BASQUE
TASTES OF THE CAMINO

SAINT-JEAN-PIED-DE-PORT

GÂTEAU BASQUE
Cream-Filled Almond Cake

Gâteau Basque is a specialty from the Basque region in southwest France. It is an almond cake with a delicate cream filling, which sometimes includes preserved cherries. I was introduced to gâteau Basque in culinary school. At first, I was not crazy about it because the particular recipe we tried was heavy on spirits. But, as I ate my way through different pastry shops in Paris, it started to grow on me. When I came back to the United States, I set out to develop a recipe I liked and was able to create one with just pastry cream and a splash of kirsch (cherry brandy) that makes an elegant, exquisite dessert. While the appearance of the cake is very simple, everyone seems quite delighted at first bite!

On the Camino Francés, you will most likely only find this cake in Saint-Jean-Pied-de-Port. So, when I was there, I made the most of my time. I had it for dessert the night before starting the Camino. I also went to a little bakery called Chez Monique on the main street of Saint-Jean-Pied-de-Port and bought two pieces for the next day: one for breakfast and one for the walk.

When I finished climbing the Pyrenées and had crossed the border between France and Spain, I took a break and had my second piece of gâteau Basque. I'm sure it gave me the energy, and even the psychological push, that I needed to start the steep descent into Roncesvalles!

Serves 8

GÂTEAU BASQUE

Cream-Filled Almond Cake

INGREDIENTS

Dough:

- 8 tablespoons (120 g) unsalted butter, softened
- 1 cup (200 g) sugar
- 2 egg yolks
- 1 tablespoon (15 ml) kirsch
- 2 teaspoons (10 ml) almond extract
- 1½ cups (190 g) all-purpose flour
- ⅓ cup (35 g) almond flour
- 1 teaspoon (5 g) baking powder
- ½ teaspoon (3 g) salt

Pastry Cream:

- 2 egg yolks
- ¼ cup (50 g) sugar
- 3 tablespoons (45 g) all-purpose flour
- 1¼ (315 ml) cups whole milk
- 1 teaspoon (5 ml) vanilla extract
- 1 egg, beaten

To prepare the dough, use a mixer to beat the butter and sugar together on medium speed until well blended. Add the egg yolks one at a time, incorporating well after each addition. Add the kirsch and almond extract. Whisk the dry ingredients (all-purpose flour, almond flour, baking powder, and salt) in a separate bowl. Reduce the speed of the mixer to low and gradually add the dry ingredients. Mix the dough until it holds together. Divide the dough into two balls and flatten out into disks. Wrap each disk of dough with plastic wrap and chill in the refrigerator until the dough is firm but malleable, about one hour.

To prepare the pastry cream, whisk the egg yolks and the sugar until frothy and light in color. Add the flour and mix these ingredients on medium speed until well combined and then set aside. Heat the milk in a medium saucepan. As soon as the milk begins to boil, take the pan off the heat. Pour half of the milk into the egg and flour mixture while whisking

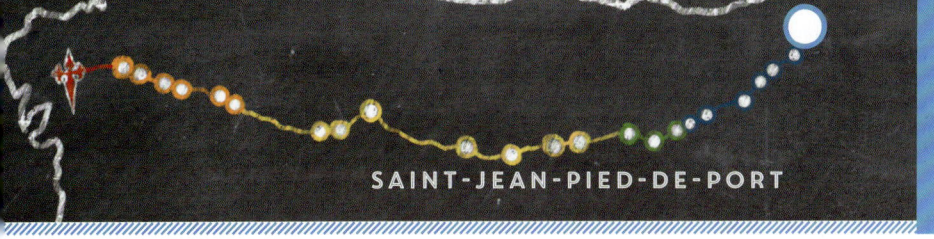

PAYS BASQUE
TASTES OF THE CAMINO

until smooth. Bring the remaining milk back to a boil, add the egg/milk mixture to the boiling milk, and continue whisking for one or two more minutes until the mixture thickens. Once it is thick enough that you can see the bottom of the pan while whisking, remove the pastry cream from the heat and add the vanilla extract. Spread the pastry cream in a shallow baking dish to cool and cover with plastic wrap placed directly on top of the pastry cream. Set aside to cool.

Preheat the oven to 350°F (180°C).

Line the bottom of a 9-inch (23 cm) round cake pan with parchment paper. Dust your work surface with some all-purpose flour and, using a rolling pin, roll out one of the disks of dough into an 11-inch (28 cm) circle. Drape the dough over the rolling pin and transfer it to the cake pan, gently pressing the dough down into the bottom and up the sides of the pan. If the dough cracks, do not worry. Just patch it up as it will not show when the cake is finally baked. Pour the pastry cream onto the dough and spread evenly.

Roll out the remaining disk of dough to make a 9-inch (23 cm) circle. Carefully place it into the cake pan, on top of the pastry cream, to form the top layer of the cake. Press the edges of the two layers together to enclose the pastry cream. With a small knife, trim off any excess dough. Using the back of a fork, draw a crosshatch pattern on top of the cake. This is the typical design of a gâteau Basque that only is filled with pastry cream. One that also contains preserved cherries would be marked with a Basque cross, which looks like a pinwheel. Brush the top of the cake with the beaten egg and place it on the center rack of the preheated oven.

Bake for about 40 to 45 minutes, or until golden brown. Remove from oven and cool for 10 to 15 minutes before inverting onto a cooling rack. Cool another 10 minutes before turning the cake right side up and letting it cool completely. Transfer to a serving plate and serve at room temperature.

Tastes of the Camino

NAVARRA

NAVARRA
TASTES OF THE CAMINO

RONCESVALLES

TRUCHA A LA NAVARRA
Navarra-Style Trout

Like the basis of many Spanish dishes, the Navarra trout reflects the conditions of the region. The Navarra region is not by the sea, but it has a lot of rivers and streams with the conditions that trout love—cold, clean, oxygen-rich water. Most of these waterways have their sources in the Pyrenées, and this makes Navarra one of the top fly-fishing regions in Spain. In addition, because cooking oil was scarce in the Pyrenées region, bacon or pork fat became the fat of choice for cooking practically everything in the region. At times, the trout is stuffed with *Serrano* ham. Along with the bacon, the richness of the Serrano ham is a very nice complement to the tenderness of the trout.

I first experienced this dish in Roncesvalles after a long day up and down the Pyrenées. I arrived in Roncesvalles set on trying to eat healthily on the Camino and opted for the lightest dish on the menu, *Trucha a la Navarra*. Of course, anyone who has done the Camino will tell you that it probably is one of the only times in your life that you can eat everything you want and you will not gain weight! But I'm so glad I tried this dish as, being full of flavor yet not too heavy, it added a nice option to my dinner repertoire back home.

Serves 4

RONCESVALLES

NAVARRA
TASTES OF THE CAMINO

TRUCHA A LA NAVARRA

Navarra-Style Trout

INGREDIENTS

- 4 fresh rainbow (or any freshwater) trout, gutted and scaled
- 1 teaspoon (5 g) pepper
- 1 teaspoon (5 g) salt
- ½ lemon, juiced
- 4 slices of Serrano ham
- 4 ounces (120 g) of bacon, diced
- 2 tablespoons (30 ml) olive oil
- 3 garlic cloves, minced
- ¼ cup (30 g) all-purpose flour
- 2 tablespoons chopped flat leaf parsley (about 4 sprigs)

Rinse each trout in cold water and pat dry. Season each trout with salt, pepper and lemon juice, inside and out. Place the trout aside for about five minutes.

In the meantime, heat a large skillet and sauté the slices of Serrano ham for about one minute or until crisp. When cool enough to handle, place one slice of the Serrano ham inside each trout. Secure each trout with wooden skewers or toothpicks to keep the ham inside it.

Heat the olive oil and cook the diced bacon until it is slightly brown and the fat disappears. Then add the garlic and cook for about 1 minute. While the bacon and garlic cook, spread the flour on a plate and lightly coat each trout with flour and set aside. Lift the diced bacon out of the skillet and set aside.

Add the trout to the skillet and pan fry it in the remaining oil. Turn carefully and fry each side until it is brown and crisp. Transfer to a serving platter and sprinkle with the diced bacon and parsley.

NAVARRA
TASTES OF THE CAMINO

AKERRETA

BACALAO AJOARRIERO
Ajoarriero-Style Salt Cod

I was introduced to this dish in Akerreta just outside of Pamplona, after a very long, wet, and muddy day full of rocky steep descents. Originally from the Navarra region, this dish is associated with the activities of *arrieros* or mule drivers, people who are hired to transport products on mules or horses. It is believed that the arrieros used salt cod as it kept well when they were constantly on the move. The other ingredients—tomatoes, garlic, and bell peppers—are thought to have been incorporated into this dish simply because they were available in the regions through which the arrieros traveled.

I like serving this dish with country bread, but you can certainly serve it with boiled or roasted potatoes. If you have difficulty finding salt cod, feel free to use fresh cod. When using fresh cod, omit the first step (de-salting the cod).

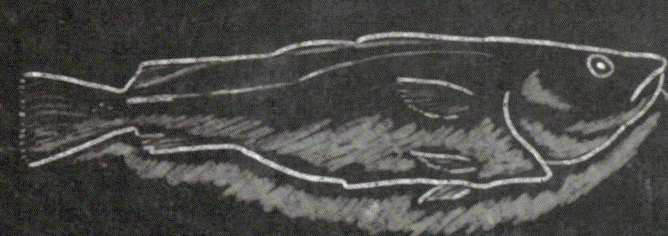

INGREDIENTS

- 2 pounds salt cod (about 1 kg), cut into 3-inch pieces
- About 3 cups (750 ml) olive oil
- 3 garlic cloves, minced
- 2 large onions, chopped
- 1 green bell pepper, sliced into thin strips
- 1 red bell pepper, sliced into thin strips
- 1 cup (250 ml) chopped tomatoes (approximately one 14-ounce can)
- 1 tablespoon (15 g) tomato paste
- Salt, pepper, and sugar to taste
- 4 large eggs, beaten
- 2 tablespoons chopped flat leaf parsley (about 4 sprigs)

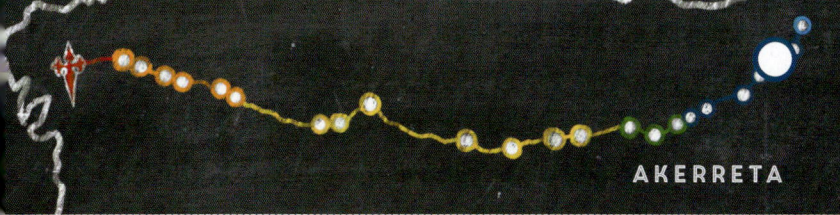

BACALAO AJOARRIERO

Ajoarriero-Style Salt Cod

Place the cod in a 9-inch x 13-inch (23 cm by 33 cm) baking dish, at least 24–36 hours prior to cooking and cover with cold water to de-salt. Place in the refrigerator and change the water every eight hours. Remove the fish from the water and pat dry.

Place the cod pieces in a large skillet (about 12 inches or 30 cm) and cover with the oil. Bring the oil to a simmer and cook the cod for about 10 minutes, until it is tender and flaky. Remove the cod from the oil and allow to cool.

In a sauté pan, heat about half a cup of oil (you can use the same oil you used to poach the cod). Add the garlic and cook it for 1–2 minutes or until it is brown and fragrant. Add the onion and the bell peppers and sauté for about 10–12 minutes, or until the vegetables are softened. Add the chopped tomatoes and tomato paste and cook for another 10 minutes. Season to taste with salt, pepper, and sugar.

While the sauce cooks, remove any skin or bones from the cod and flake it with a fork. When the sauce is ready, add the cod to the pan. Mix the cod thoroughly with the sauce and cook for about 10 minutes. Add the beaten eggs to the cod and cook for another 2–3 minutes. Top with the chopped parsley and serve immediately.

NAVARRA
TASTES OF THE CAMINO

PAMPLONA

HUEVOS ROTOS CON SERRANO Y PATATAS

Broken Eggs with Serrano Ham and Potatoes

Huevos rotos literally means "broken eggs." They are fried eggs that are traditionally served over French fries. Just before serving, the egg yolks are broken with the tip of a knife and the yolks ooze all over the fries. Unlike in the United States, eggs are rarely eaten for breakfast in Spain. Rather, they are commonly eaten at lunch or dinner.

I had huevos rotos on both of my journeys along the Camino Francés, but my favorites were the ones I had on my second Camino at Café Iruña in Pamplona. We had walked in cold, wet conditions that day and we were looking for simple, but filling, hot food. This dish totally fit the bill! The reason these were my favorite is that they were prepared with roasted potatoes rather than with fries—and they contained strips of Serrano ham that had been crisped in a skillet. Upon my return to the United States, I took this recipe further by roasting onions together with the potatoes and adding piquillo peppers.

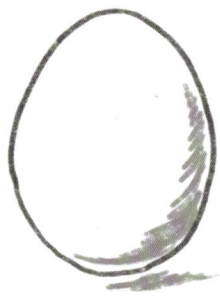

Serves 4

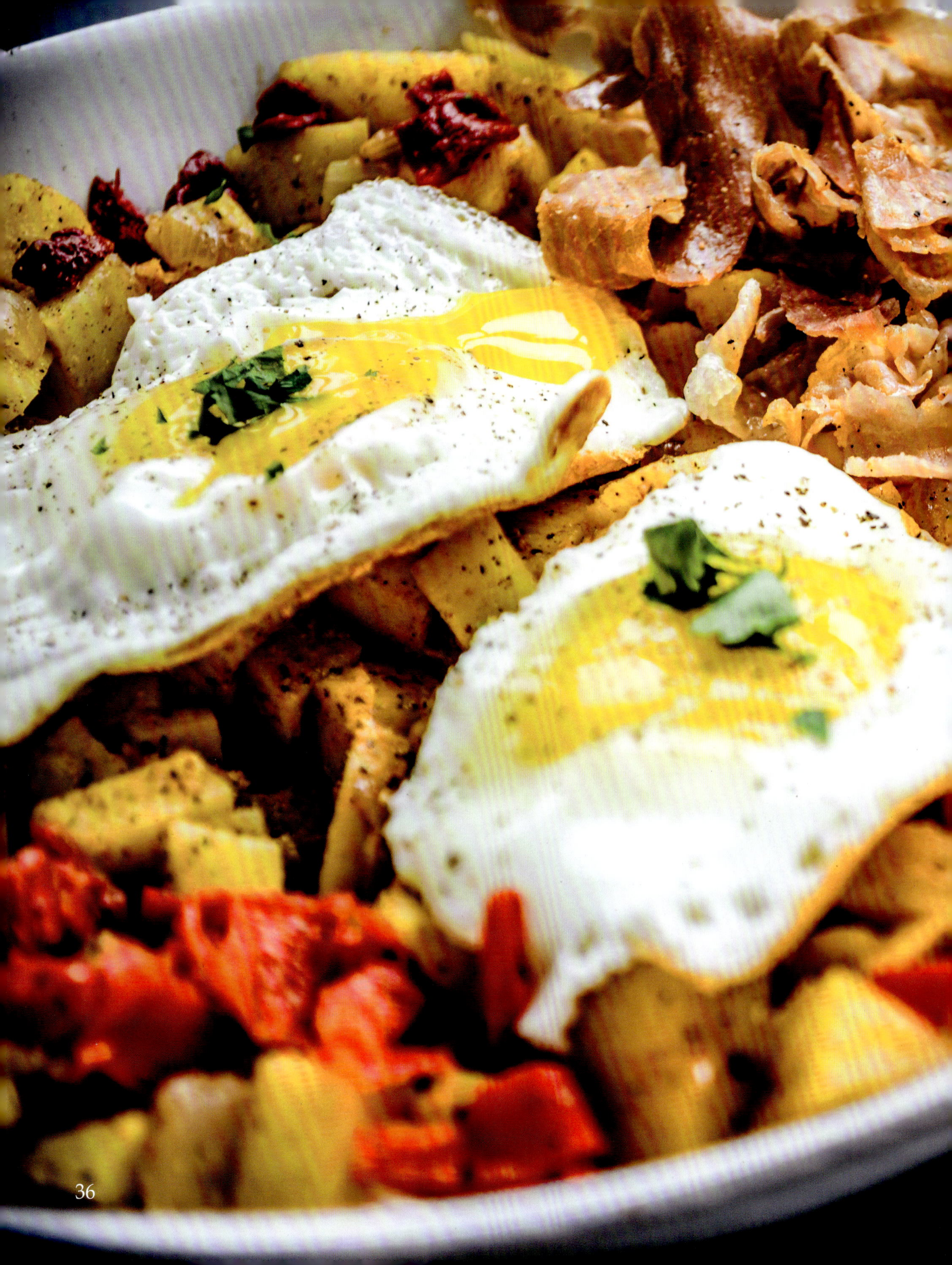

NAVARRA
TASTES OF THE CAMINO

PAMPLONA

HUEVOS ROTOS CON SERRANO Y PATATAS

Broken Eggs with Serrano Ham and Potatoes

INGREDIENTS

- 4 medium potatoes (preferably Yukon gold), peeled and cut into ½-inch cubes
- 1 large onion, finely chopped
- 6 garlic cloves, minced
- ¼ cup (60 ml) olive oil
- 2 teaspoons (10 g) salt
- 1 teaspoon (5 g) pepper
- 1 teaspoon (3 g) mild (*dulce*) Spanish paprika
- 1 teaspoon (5 g) sugar
- 8 slices of Serrano ham, sliced into small strips
- 2 piquillo peppers, sliced into small strips
- 8 large eggs
- 2 tablespoons chopped flat leaf parsley (about 4 sprigs), for garnishing

Preheat the oven to 400°F (200°C.)

Mix the potatoes, onion, garlic, olive oil, salt, pepper, paprika, and sugar in a bowl and spread onto a baking sheet. Roast for about 20 minutes or until tender, turning the potatoes half way through the baking time.

In the meantime, pan fry the Serrano ham for about 3–5 minutes, just enough to make it crisp. In the same skillet, heat the piquillo peppers briefly and set aside. When the potatoes are ready, taste and add more salt and pepper if necessary. Mix the Serrano and the piquillo peppers with the potatoes and divide among four deep plates.

Pour some olive oil into the skillet and fry the eggs over easy—each egg should be turned over when the white is nearly done and fried lightly on the other side, so that the yolk remains slightly liquid. Serve two eggs on each plate with the potatoes, sprinkle with sea salt and parsley, and break the yolks with the tip of the knife right before eating.

NAVARRA
TASTES OF THE CAMINO

PUENTE LA REINA

SOPA DE LENTEJAS

Lentil Soup

Lentil soup is found all along the Camino as it is a hearty, filling soup, perfect for a hungry, tired pilgrim. In addition, lentils are high in protein, iron, and dietary fiber, making this soup inexpensively nutritious.

I first ate lentil soup in the restaurant of the Hotel Jakué in Puente La Reina after having slowly and steadily climbed to the *Alto del Perdón*—the Peak of Forgiveness. After having reached this "forgiveness peak," once in scalding heat of 39°C (or 102°F) and another time with mud up to my ankles, I felt like I could be somewhat gluttonous and treat myself to multiple servings of this soup. Fortunately, the meal was served buffet style.

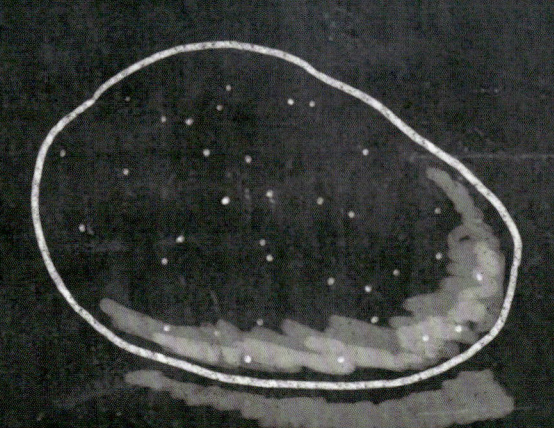

Serves 8-10

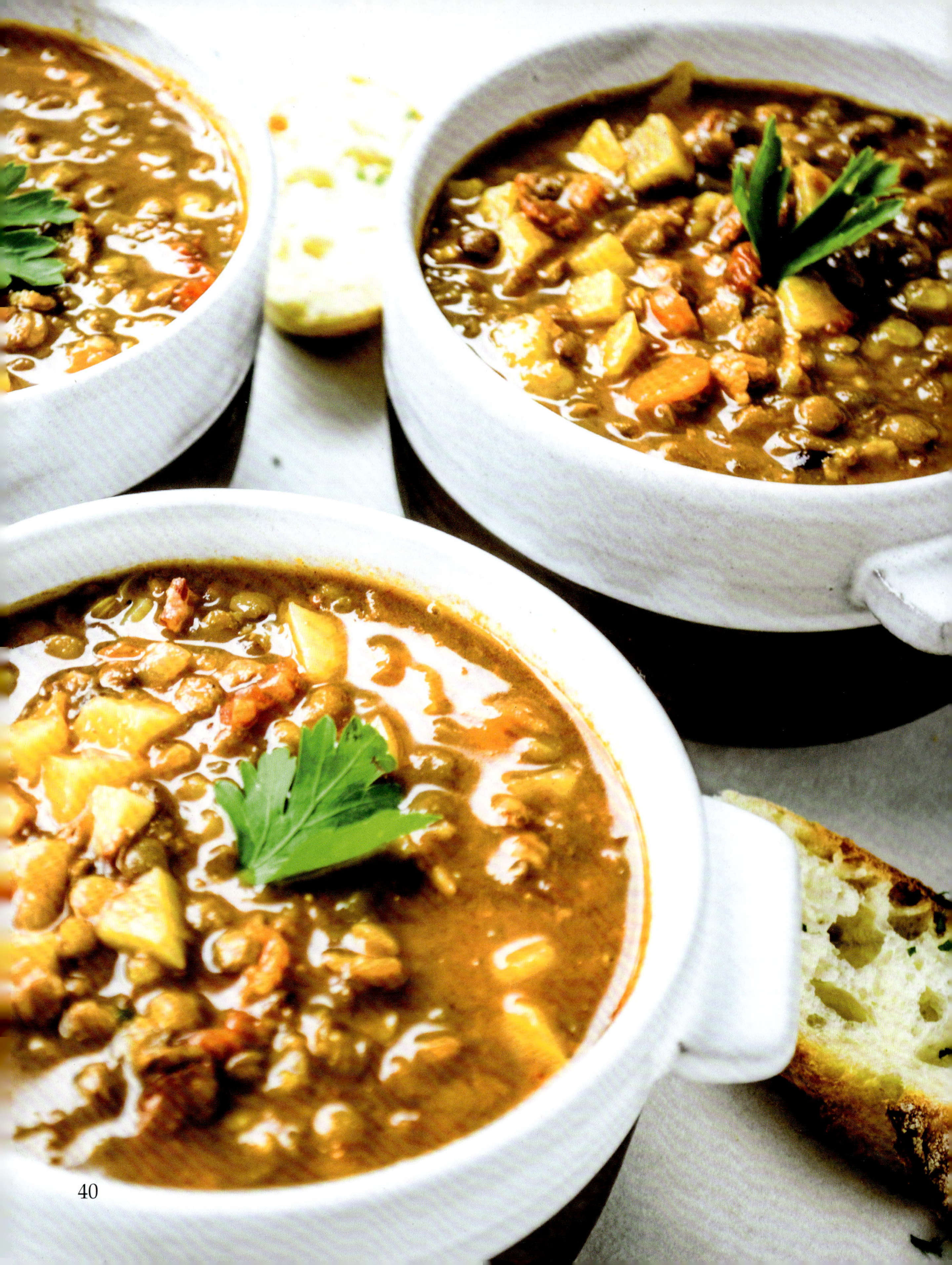

PUENTE LA REINA

NAVARRA
TASTES OF THE CAMINO

SOPA DE LENTEJAS
Lentil Soup

INGREDIENTS

- 2 cups (250 g) brown lentils
- 8 cups (2 l) chicken stock
- ¼ cup (60 ml) olive oil
- 1 large onion, chopped
- 1 large carrot, chopped
- 4 garlic cloves, minced
- 4 ounces (120 g) bacon, diced
- 1 cup chopped tomatoes
- 1 teaspoon (3 g) mild (*dulce*) Spanish paprika
- 1 medium potato, peeled and finely diced
- 1 tablespoon (15 g) tomato paste
- 2–3 bay leaves
- Salt and pepper to taste

Rinse the lentils in cold water and pick them over for tiny stones. In a stock pot (6–8 quarts / liters), bring the stock to a boil and add the lentils. Simmer for about 15 minutes.

In the meantime, in a large skillet, heat the olive oil over medium heat. Add the onion and carrot and, after 1 minute, reduce the heat to low. Cook until the onion is soft and golden, approximately 5–7 minutes. Add the garlic and the bacon and stir well for about a minute. Then add the tomatoes and the paprika and cook for another 2–3 minutes. Season the vegetables with salt and pepper to taste.

Add the vegetable mixture to the lentils along with the potato, tomato paste, and bay leaves. Simmer, covered, for about 25–30 minutes, or until the lentils are softened. Season with salt and pepper to taste, and serve.

NAVARRA
TASTES OF THE CAMINO

LOS ARCOS

PERAS AL VINO TINTO
Poached Pears in Red Wine

Because I love to cook, I'm frequently asked if I grew up cooking with my mother or grandmother. Unfortunately, I was raised far away from both of my grandmothers. As for my mother, she really does not enjoy cooking—or baking—to this day. However, she entertains with an elegance rarely found elsewhere and she has a few tried and true dishes that she resorts to when she *must* cook. One of her signature desserts is *Peras al Vino Tinto*. While I did not enjoy fruit desserts as a child, I remember thinking how beautifully she plated the pears with vanilla ice cream and a mint leaf before serving them to her guests.

As I was walking on the red clay and through the vineyards just past Los Arcos, right before entering the Rioja region, it occurred to me that, as a tribute to the great red wines of the region (as well as to my mother), I had to feature the pears in this book. In Spain, it is customary to end a meal with fruit, and this light dessert is the perfect follow-up to a rich main course. Of course, if "lightness" is not your thing, feel free to serve the pears with ice cream.

Serves 8

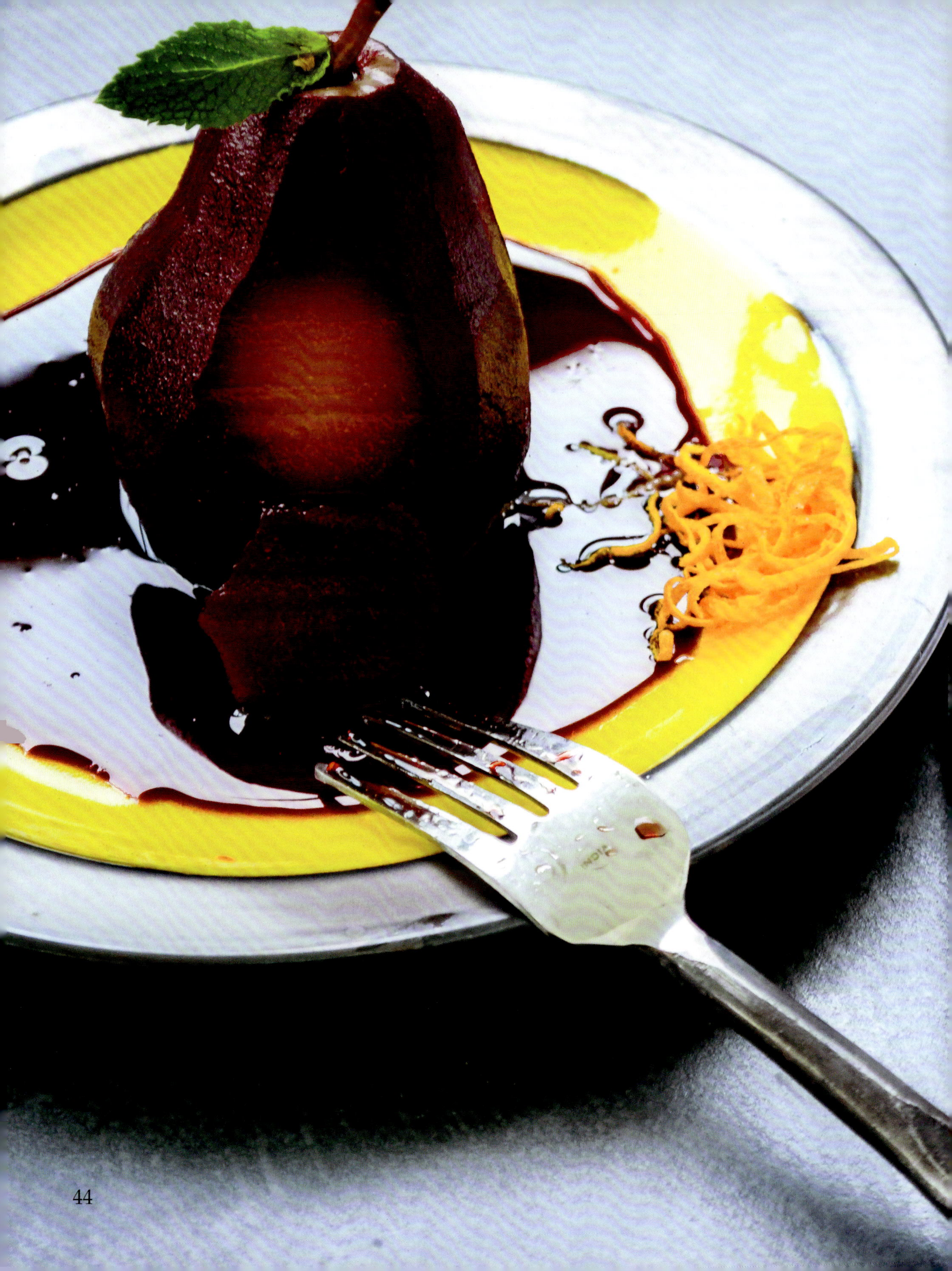

NAVARRA
TASTES OF THE CAMINO

LOS ARCOS

PERAS AL VINO TINTO
Poached Pears in Red Wine

INGREDIENTS

- 8 small, firm pears (Bosc, Anjou, or Bartlett will work)
- 3 cups red Rioja wine (one 750 ml bottle)
- 1 cup (200 g) sugar
- Zest of one medium orange
- 1 cinnamon stick
- 1 vanilla bean, split lengthwise
- 6 black peppercorns
- 1 clove
- 8 mint leaves, for garnish

Peel the pears, leaving the stem intact, and cut the bottom ⅛-inch off each pear to create a base. Using a melon baller, scoop out balls of flesh from the bottom center of each pear. Continue scooping until all of the core and seeds are removed. The pears should look whole on the outside but hollow inside.

Pour the wine in a 6-8 qt. pot. Add the sugar, orange zest, cinnamon stick, and vanilla bean. Tie the peppercorns and clove into a piece of cheesecloth and add to the pot. Bring to a boil and simmer for five minutes.

Add the fruit to the syrup, cover the pot and simmer gently for about 20–25 minutes or until the fruit can easily be pierced with a skewer. The time on this may vary—the riper the fruit, the less time it will take to reach this point. If the pears are not totally submerged in the wine, you will have to turn them at the half way mark to ensure you get an even color. After the fruit has cooked through, allow the pears to cool in the syrup. Plate the pears and garnish with mint leaves. Serve warm, cold, or at room temperature.

NAVARRA
TASTES OF THE CAMINO

VIANA

GAMBAS AL AJILLO
Garlic Shrimp

Typically, I do not enjoy eating a full lunch until I am done walking. However, on my first Camino, as we were approaching the town of Viana, I crossed paths with an old local man who told me that we had arrived just in time for the *encierre*. According to him, the "encierre" was basically a closing or a blocking off of the town center so the cows and bulls could run free. This very basic explanation intrigued me, so I pressed him for more details. We happened to have arrived on the feast of the *Virgen de La Nieve*, a celebration that traditionally takes place after the harvest. The town celebrates in a way similar to the festival of *San Fermin* in Pamplona. The people dress up all in white (perfectly starched whites, I must say) with red sashes, and hold a mini running of the bulls, in addition to dancing the day and night away. During the running of the bulls, access to the historic city center is blocked. Nobody can enter and nobody can leave, because the bulls have taken control of the city center streets. And, for obvious reasons, you cannot be strolling down the streets, so you have to wait inside the confines of a local establishment.

Since we were sort of "trapped" in Viana, we decided to sit down for a nice and leisurely lunch at the restaurant adjacent to the Hotel Palacio de Las Pujadas while getting a glimpse of the festivities. We ordered a bunch of amazing dishes including these *gambas al ajillo*—garlic shrimp. The day had been sunny and glorious and we could not have asked for a better lunch.

Serves 4 as a main dish, or 6 as an appetizer

48

NAVARRA
TASTES OF THE CAMINO

VIANA

GAMBAS AL AJILLO
Garlic Shrimp

INGREDIENTS

- 2 lbs (about 1 kg) raw shrimp, shelled and deveined
- ¾ cup (190 ml) olive oil
- 6 garlic cloves, finely chopped
- 1 teaspoon (5 g) chili flakes
- 1 teaspoon (3 g) mild (dulce) Spanish paprika
- 2 tablespoons chopped flat leaf parsley (about 4 sprigs)
- Salt and pepper to taste
- Rustic bread for serving

Season the shrimp with salt and pepper.

Heat the oil to medium in a large sauté pan and add the garlic. Cook the garlic for about 1 minute, or until it starts turning light brown.

Immediately add the shrimp, the chili flakes, and the paprika and cook over medium heat, stirring briskly for about 3–4 minutes or until the shrimp turn pink and curl. Season with salt and pepper to taste.

Transfer to a serving platter and sprinkle with parsley. Serve with rustic bread for dipping into the garlic oil.

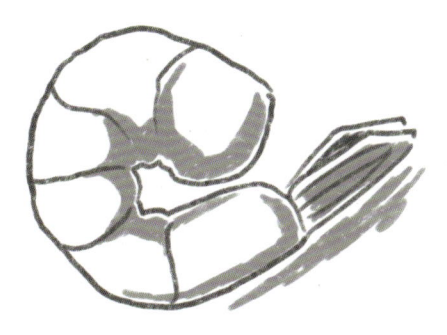

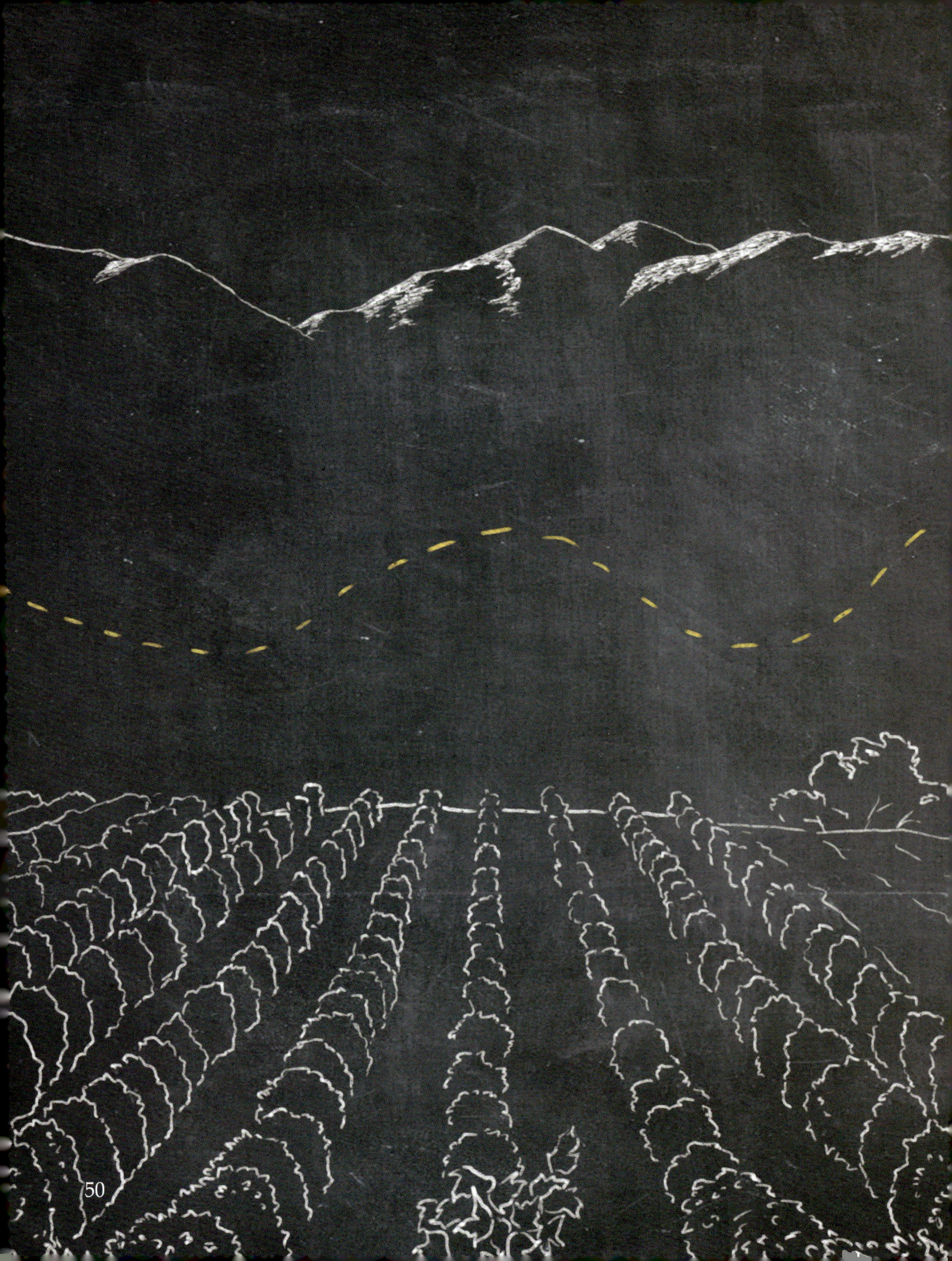

TASTES OF THE CAMINO

LA RIOJA

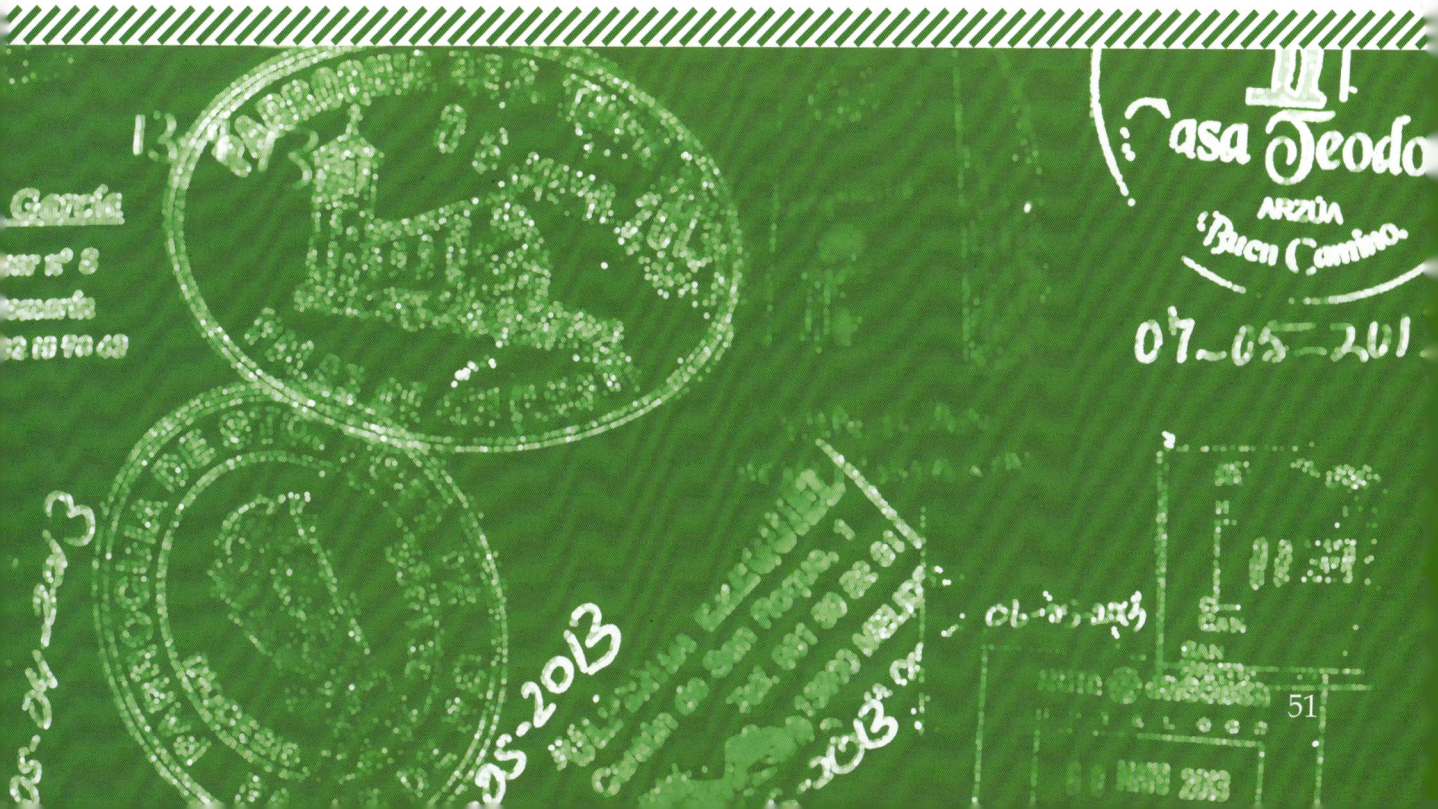

LA RIOJA
TASTES OF THE CAMINO

LOGROÑO

MELLIJONES CON SALSA DE PIMIENTOS DE PIQUILLO

Mussels with Piquillo Pepper Sauce

Unlike most mussels, these mussels are prepared with a touch of cream, creating a richer and more filling dish. I first had this dish in a tapas bar in Logroño.

I had had a good lunch prior to walking into the capital of Rioja. Hence, I was not too hungry to order a full pilgrim's menu at dinner. My mother and I bumped into a few pilgrim friends and we wandered through the streets of Logroño until we stumbled upon Bar La Fontana, where we had some great tapas and wine. I ordered these mussels and loved them so much I ended up ordering one more portion.

Serves 4–6

INGREDIENTS

- ½ cup (125 ml) olive oil
- 1 medium onion, finely chopped
- 4 garlic cloves, pressed
- 12 piquillo peppers or 6 red bell peppers, roasted, peeled, seeded, and coarsely chopped
- 4 tablespoons (32 g) all-purpose flour
- 1½ cups (375 ml) seafood stock
- 1 tablespoon (15 g) tomato paste
- 2 teaspoons (6 g) mild (dulce) Spanish paprika
- ½ teaspoon (2 g) cayenne pepper
- 2 teaspoons (10 g) salt
- 1 teaspoon (5 g) sugar
- 1 teaspoon (5 g) black pepper
- ½ cup (125 ml) cream
- 1 cup (250 ml) water
- ½ cup (125 ml) white wine
- 2 lbs (about 1 kg) mussels, scrubbed and de-bearded

LA RIOJA
TASTES OF THE CAMINO

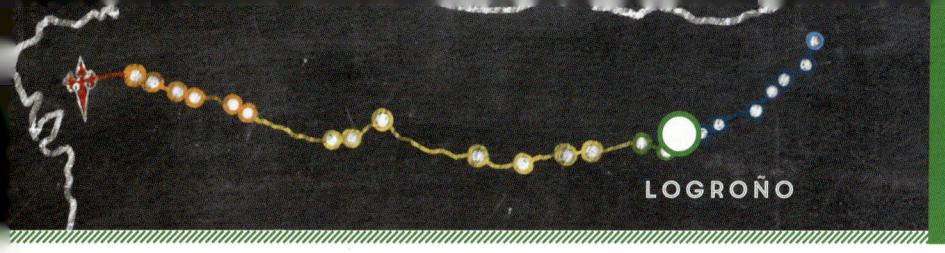

LOGROÑO

MELLIJONES CON SALSA DE PIMIENTOS DE PIQUILLO

Mussels with Piquillo Pepper Sauce

Heat a large saucepan over medium heat. Add the olive oil and cook the onion until translucent and softened. Add the garlic and the piquillo peppers and cook for about 3–5 minutes. Sprinkle the flour over the garlic-pepper mixture and mix well. Add the stock and bring to a boil. Lower heat and simmer, uncovered, for 4–5 minutes. Add the tomato paste, paprika, cayenne, salt, sugar, and black pepper.

With an immersion blender, process until smooth. If you do not have an immersion blender, you can also use a traditional blender—but be careful about overloading your blender with hot liquid. Simply transfer the pepper mixture to the blender in batches and then add them back to the pot. Once the pepper mixture has been processed until completely smooth, add the cream and heat the sauce slightly, without allowing it to boil. Adjust the seasoning (salt, pepper, and sugar) if necessary, and bring back to simmer.

Discard any mussels that are cracked or are open and won't close up when lightly tapped. Pour the water and the wine into a large pan and bring to a boil. Add the mussels, reduce the heat to medium, and cover the pan. Allow the mussels to steam open, which should take about 3–5 minutes. Remove the mussels from the pot and discard any mussels that did not open up during the cooking process. Place the mussels on a platter and generously ladle the red pepper sauce on top of them.

Make it ahead: You can make the sauce a day or two in advance, as long as you don't add the cream. Just before cooking the mussels, warm up the sauce and add the cream, then proceed as usual.

LA RIOJA
TASTES OF THE CAMINO

NÁJERA

PIMIENTOS DE PIQUILLO RELLENOS DE BACALAO CON SALSA ESPAÑOLA

Piquillo Peppers filled with Salt Cod and Spanish Sauce

I first had this dish in Nájera in a restaurant by the river called Los Parrales. Piquillo peppers are delicate peppers that are slightly sweet and have no heat. They are about three inches long and derive their name from the word for "small beak" in Spanish. They grow predominantly in the Navarra region, but have become popular throughout Spain and beyond. The harvest takes place in either September or December but because they are invariably preserved in brine, they are available as a shelf-stable item all year long.

The peppers are handpicked and roasted over coals, and then peeled and deseeded by hand before being packed in jars. Piquillos are frequently stuffed with seafood or meat and served as tapas in small *cazuelas* (Spanish clay deep dishes). If you have difficulty finding salt cod, feel free to use fresh cod. When using fresh cod, omit the first step (de-salting the cod).

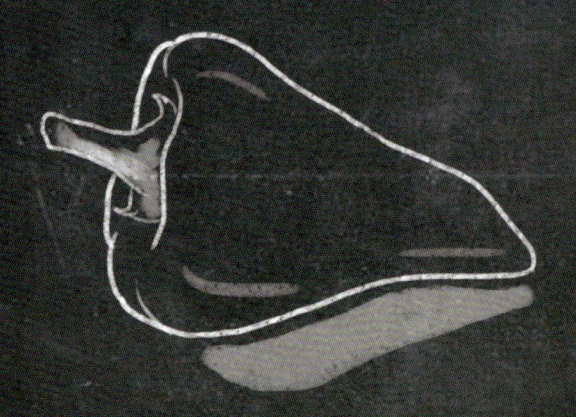

Serves 4

PIMIENTOS DE PIQUILLO RELLENOS DE BACALAO CON SALSA ESPAÑOLA

Piquillo Peppers filled with Salt Cod and Spanish Sauce

INGREDIENTS

Cod filling:
- ½ pound (250 g) salt cod
- 2 tablespoons (30 ml) olive oil
- ½ onion, finely chopped
- 1 garlic clove, pressed

Béchamel sauce:
- 1 tablespoon (15 g) butter
- 2 tablespoons (30 g) all-purpose flour
- 1 cup (250 ml) whole milk
- Salt, pepper, and nutmeg, to taste

Spanish sauce:
- 4 tablespoons (60 ml) olive oil
- 1 small onion, finely chopped
- 1 medium carrot, finely sliced
- 4 tablespoons (30 g) all-purpose flour
- 4 cups (1 l) beef stock
- 1 tablespoon (15 g) tomato paste
- 3 garlic cloves, finely chopped
- 1 bay leaf
- ¼ teaspoon dried thyme
- 1½ tablespoon (22 ml) dry sherry
- Salt and pepper, to taste

10–12 roasted piquillo peppers (a 12 oz jar)

LA RIOJA
TASTES OF THE CAMINO

NÁJERA

Place the salt cod in a baking dish and soak in cold water for 24–36 hours, changing the water every eight hours. Once the cod has been desalted, shred it into flakes and set aside.

Heat the olive oil in a medium skillet. Add the onion and sauté until soft and translucent. Add the garlic and cook 1 more minute. Then add the shredded cod and cook for 3–5 minutes. Set aside and let cool while you prepare the béchamel sauce.

In a small saucepan (about 1 or 2 quarts/liters), melt the butter over medium heat and then add the flour. Whisk until the flour is fully incorporated into the butter and forms a thick paste. Pour in the milk and whisk until it becomes thickened. Remove the béchamel sauce from the heat and add to the cod mixture, blending thoroughly. Season with salt, pepper, and nutmeg to taste.

While the cod-béchamel mixture cools down and sets, prepare the Spanish sauce. In a medium saucepan (about 3 quarts/liters), heat the olive oil and add the onion and the carrot, stirring occasionally until they are softened. Add the flour and blend well with the vegetables. Add the stock and whisk vigorously to avoid lumps. Add the tomato paste, garlic, bay leaf, and thyme and bring to a boil. Reduce to a simmer and cook for about 40 minutes to blend the flavors. Stir in the sherry and simmer for 3 minutes. Pass through a sieve into a bowl and discard the solids. Season to taste with salt and pepper and keep warm while you fill the peppers.

Preheat the oven to 300°F (150°C).

Drain the piquillo peppers carefully, so as not to tear them. Gently hold each pepper in one hand and fill it up with about two teaspoons of the cod-béchamel mixture. Then set the filled peppers in a baking dish. Put the peppers in the oven for about 10–15 minutes, or long enough to heat through. Spoon the Spanish sauce over the peppers and serve.

LA RIOJA
TASTES OF THE CAMINO

SANTO DOMINGO DE LA CALZADA

CROQUETAS DE JAMÓN SERRANO

Serrano Ham Croquettes

I have eaten many *croquetas* in my life—at kids' birthday parties, at cocktail parties, at tapas bars, when visiting my great aunts, etc., but one of the best croquetas I ever had was in Santo Domingo de la Calzada at a bar called La Piedra, just half a block from the cathedral. These croquetas were creamy inside, crunchy outside, and intensely flavorful throughout. They inspired me to develop this recipe.

Traditionally, croquetas are made with regular fine breadcrumbs. But, in this recipe, I deviate a bit from tradition and use Panko (Japanese) breadcrumbs, which are really flaky and add a lovely texture and crunchiness to the croquetas. When I entertain, I typically will make two or three types of croquetas (cod, ham, chicken, etc.). I shape each flavor differently, some in small balls and some in small logs, so my guests can tell the difference.

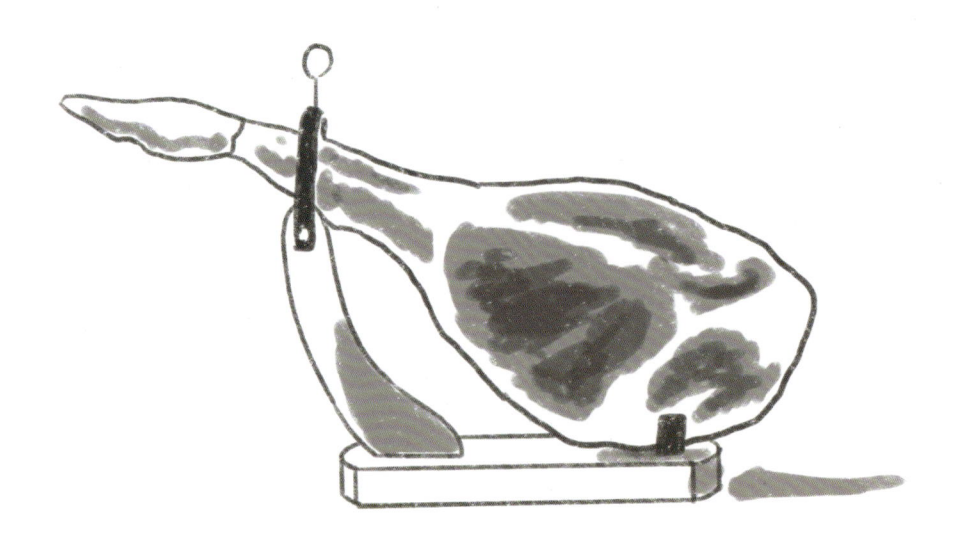

Makes about 60 croquetas →

61

CROQUETAS DE JAMÓN SERRANO

Serrano Ham Croquettes

INGREDIENTS

- 2 tablespoons (30 ml) olive oil
- 1 medium onion, finely chopped
- 1 garlic clove, finely chopped
- 8 oz (240 g) Serrano ham, finely shredded
- 6 tablespoons (90 g) butter
- 2½ cups (320 g) all-purpose flour, divided
- 2½ cups (625 ml) whole milk
- Salt, pepper, and nutmeg to taste
- 3 large eggs, beaten
- 2–3 cups (120-180 g) Panko breadcrumbs
- 2–3 cups (500–750 ml) canola or grapeseed oil for deep frying

Heat the olive oil in a medium skillet. Add the onion and sauté until soft and translucent, about 5 minutes. Add the garlic and cook 1 more minute. Then add the shredded ham and set aside to cool while you prepare the béchamel sauce.

In a medium saucepan, melt the butter and then add one cup (125g) of flour. Whisk until the flour is fully incorporated into the butter and forms a thick paste. Pour in the milk and whisk constantly over medium heat until it becomes very thick (this usually takes about 5 minutes). When it is ready, the sauce will pull away from the edges of the pan and you will be able to see the bottom of the pan as you whisk it. Add the ham mixture to the béchamel sauce and blend thoroughly. Season with salt, pepper, and nutmeg to taste. Pour into a baking

SANTO DOMINGO DE LA CALZADA

LA RIOJA
TASTES OF THE CAMINO

dish, cover with plastic wrap and allow to cool for at least 2 hours, or overnight.

Place three shallow bowls/plates next to each other. Place the remaining 1½ cups (195 g) of flour in one, the beaten eggs in the next, and the Panko breadcrumbs in the third. To form the croquetas, take small portions of the béchamel mixture and shape them into small rounds. I like using a truffle scoop—like an ice cream scoop, but smaller—to keep the size consistent, or you can use a melon baller. First roll the rounds in the flour, then in the egg, and finally in the Panko breadcrumbs. Set the prepared croquetas on a baking sheet. When done breading all of the croquetas, place them in the refrigerator for at least 30 minutes to set before frying.

Heat the oil to medium in a deep skillet or pot. Carefully lower the croquetas into the oil to avoid splattering, and fry them for about 5 minutes or until they are lightly browned. Lift them with a slotted spoon and place on paper towels to drain. Fry them in batches and do not overcrowd the pot as overcrowding will decrease the temperature of the oil and cause the croquetas to take longer to cook and absorb more oil in the process. Serve immediately, or keep in an oven heated to 200°F until ready to serve.

Make it ahead: Once you have breaded the croquetas, you can freeze them, stored in an airtight container, and take them out and thaw them when you are ready to fry them.

64

TASTES OF THE CAMINO

CASTILLA Y LÉON

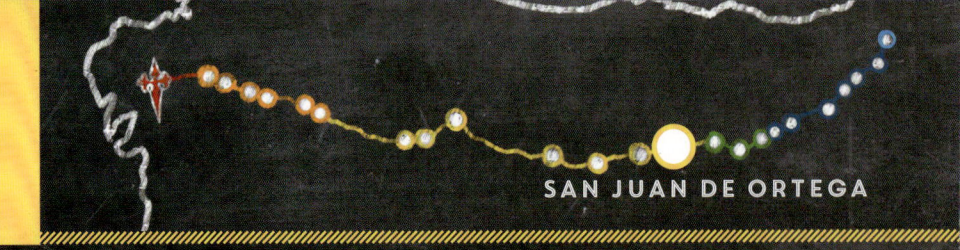

CASTILLA Y LÉON
TASTES OF THE CAMINO

SAN JUAN DE ORTEGA

SOPA DE AJO
Garlic Soup

I first heard of this soup as I approached San Juan de Ortega. For many years, a local priest would serve this soup to all pilgrims after the evening mass. Supposedly, the tradition was kept up even after the priest passed away in 2008.

Unfortunately, on both occasions when I was in San Juan de Ortega, there was no garlic soup to be found, so I was left wondering what exactly was this famous soup. Somewhere between San Juan de Ortega and Burgos, I saw it listed on a menu easel outside a small bar. I went in and tried it, and have been hooked on it ever since. Essentially, it is peasant food in its purest form. It is a simple soup consisting of garlic, crusty country bread, and eggs. While one would think this would be a thin, watery soup, the bread and the eggs give it substance and body. It's great for chilly nights when you are looking for something comforting and simple.

Serves 4

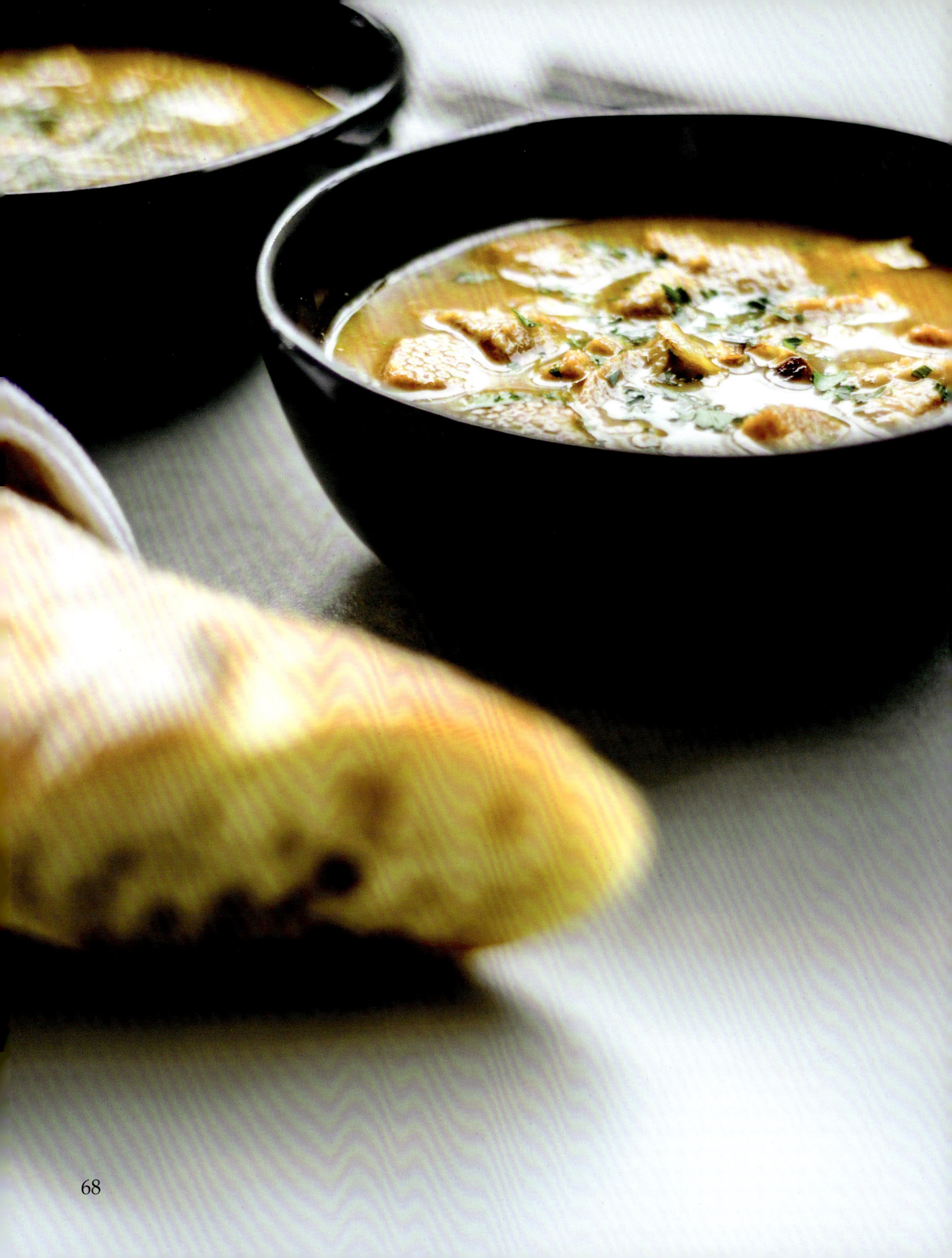

SAN JUAN DE ORTEGA

CASTILLA Y LÉON
TASTES OF THE CAMINO

SOPA DE AJO

Garlic Soup

INGREDIENTS

- 2 tablespoons (30 ml) olive oil
- 10 garlic cloves, peeled
- 6 slices (¼-inch (½-cm) thick) of country bread, cut into cubes
- 1 bay leaf
- 1 teaspoon (3 g) mild (dulce) Spanish paprika
- 4–5 cups (1–1.25 l) beef stock
- 4 large eggs, lightly beaten
- Salt and pepper to taste
- 1 tablespoon chopped flat leaf parsley (about 2 sprigs), for garnish.

In a medium saucepan, heat the olive oil to medium and then add the peeled garlic cloves. Sauté them gently until soft and remove from the pan. Crush the garlic in a mortar and pestle—or put through a garlic press—and set aside. Add the pieces of bread to the pan and toast them lightly. Add the garlic back into the pot with the bread, along with the bay leaf, paprika, and 4 cups of stock and simmer for about 10 minutes. Increase the heat and gradually pour the beaten eggs into the soup, whisking constantly until the eggs have set. If the soup is too thick, add an additional ½–1 cup (125–250 ml) of stock. Season with salt and pepper to taste. Ladle the soup into bowls and garnish with the finely chopped parsley.

CASTILLA Y LÉON

TASTES OF THE CAMINO

BURGOS

LECHE FRITA

Fried Milk

After having settled into our accommodation in Burgos, I was on the hunt for a nice restaurant for dinner. I had only had a bowl of soup all day and was starving. In addition, we were in one of the largest cities along the Camino and I wanted to take a break from the traditional *menú de peregrino*. Mesón El Cid, situated right in front of the cathedral, had been highly recommended and I decided to splurge a bit. Each course was divine, but the course that really caught my eye was dessert. I had never heard of *Leche Frita*, which is essentially a thick custard that has been sliced, breaded, and pan fried.

While the rendition at Mesón El Cid was a bit sophisticated—it was flambéed for us at the table—I really enjoyed the traditional versions commonly found in pastry shops along the Camino, which are portable and make great snacks. While I prefer them while still warm, I had my fair share of them at room temperature on the Camino and can assure you they will make any pilgrim happy. In addition, I like to vary the type of breadcrumbs depending on the texture I'm looking for. Fine breadcrumbs create a smoother, more refined product, while coarser crumbs create an amazing contrast of texture against the smooth filling.

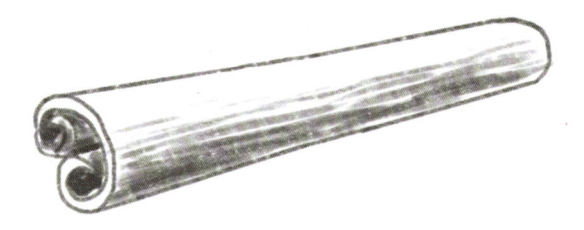

Serves 8

INGREDIENTS

- 2 cups (500 ml) whole milk, divided (using low-fat milk will yield a poor result)
- Zest of one orange, finely grated
- 1 cinnamon stick
- ⅓ cup (40 g) cornstarch
- 5 large eggs, divided
- ½ cup (100 g) sugar
- 1 teaspoon (5 ml) vanilla
- 1 cup (125 g) all-purpose flour
- 1 cup (90 g) bread crumbs
- 1–1½ cups (250–325 ml) neutral oil (grape seed, sunflower, etc.), for frying
- ¼ cup (30 g) powdered sugar
- 2 teaspoons (6 g) ground cinnamon
- Mint leaves or fresh raspberries for garnish (optional)

BURGOS

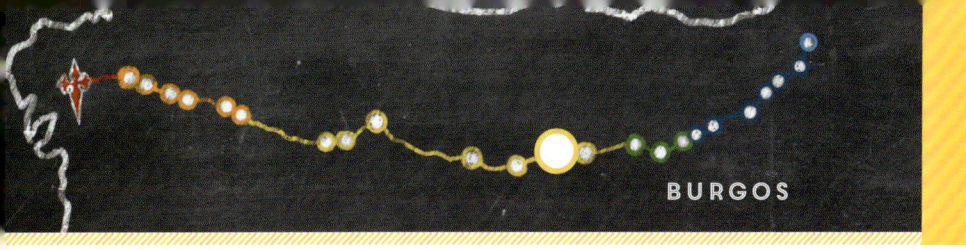

CASTILLA Y LÉON

TASTES OF THE CAMINO

LECHE FRITA

Fried Milk

In a medium saucepan, boil 1½ cups (375 ml) of milk, orange zest, and cinnamon stick. While the milk comes to a boil, whisk the cornstarch into the remaining ½ cup (125 ml) of milk, whisking vigorously until smooth. In a separate bowl, whisk three eggs with the sugar and then stir in the cornstarch mixture.

When the milk has come to a boil, remove the cinnamon stick and gradually pour half of the boiling milk into the egg mixture while whisking continuously. This will elevate the temperature of the eggs and should prevent them from curdling when added to the hot milk. Return the egg mixture to the pan with the remaining hot milk. Whisk constantly until you have a thick and smooth cream, about 10-15 minutes. Remove the pan from the heat and add the vanilla.

Using a pastry brush, oil the inside of an 8-inch x 8-inch (20-cm x 20-cm) square baking dish and spread the cream mixture in it. Allow to cool for a few minutes, cover with plastic wrap laid directly on the surface of the cream, and chill for a few hours or overnight.

Once the cream has chilled, whisk the remaining two eggs in a small bowl. Place the breadcrumbs and the flour in separate shallow dishes. Cut the chilled custard into squares (2 inches by 2 inches or 5 cm by 5 cm). Coat each piece in flour, then dip in the egg, and finally coat in breadcrumbs.

Heat about a half inch of oil in a medium skillet and pan fry each custard square until golden brown on both sides. Remove from the skillet and drain on paper towels. Mix the powdered sugar with the cinnamon and sprinkle on the fried custard.

Two squares make a good serving size. Garnish with mint leaves or fresh raspberries, if so desired. Serve warm.

CASTILLA Y LÉON
TASTES OF THE CAMINO

CASTROJERIZ

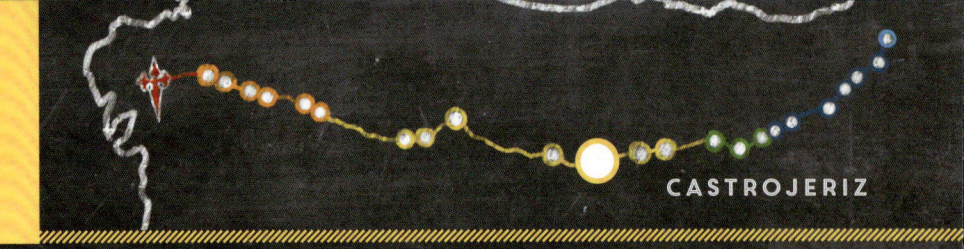

FLAN DE LECHE

Crème Caramel

Flan is a typical dessert option on the *menú de peregrinos* and I certainly ate more than my fair share of it along the Camino. Growing up in South America, I was practically raised on flan, and I am incredibly particular when it comes to this dessert. Along the way, many pilgrim menus feature a bland, store-bought flan that leaves much to be desired. But there was one particular restaurant, El Mesón in Castrojeriz, which served homemade flan (or, as they say in Spanish, "de la casa") and it met all my criteria for an exceptional flan. The end result resembled the flan recipe that I enjoyed as a child and which I share here.

Serves 8–10

INGREDIENTS

- 1¾ cup (350 g) sugar, divided
- ½ cup water
- 2 cups (500 ml) whole milk (using low-fat milk will yield a poor result)
- 1 cinnamon stick
- 1 2-inch (5 cm) strip orange peel
- 1 teaspoon salt
- 6 large eggs
- 1 tablespoon (15 ml) vanilla extract

CASTROJERIZ

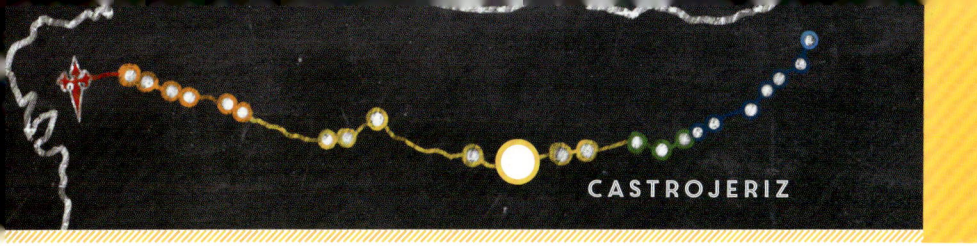

CASTILLA Y LÉON

TASTES OF THE CAMINO

FLAN DE LECHE

Crème Caramel

In a small saucepan, mix 1 cup (200 g) of sugar and the water and cook over medium-low heat, swirling the pan occasionally, until it caramelizes, becoming golden amber in color. The whole process of preparing the caramel can take about 20 minutes. It will seem slow, initially, but once the sugar starts turning color, it speeds up considerably and can quickly turn too dark—or even burn. Because of this, you must monitor the cooking closely.

Pour the caramel into an 8-inch (20-cm) flan mold or Bundt pan while quickly turning and tilting the mold to coat the bottom and the sides of the mold. The caramel will solidify almost immediately once you pour it in the pan. This is perfectly normal. Set aside.

Preheat the oven to 350°F (180°C).

In a saucepan, mix the milk, cinnamon stick, orange peel, and salt and bring to a boil. While the milk mixture is coming to a boil, beat the eggs with the remaining ¾ cup (150 g) of sugar and the vanilla.

When the milk has boiled, remove and discard the cinnamon stick and orange peel. Slowly add the milk to the egg mixture while whisking the eggs constantly. Adding the milk too fast will cause the eggs to curdle.

Pour this mixture into the caramel-coated mold and cover with aluminum foil. Place the mold in a roasting pan and fill the roasting pan with water until the water reaches halfway up the sides of the mold, creating a water bath. Place in the oven and bake for about 90 minutes.

Remove the mold from the water bath and refrigerate for at least 4 hours or, preferably, overnight. To serve the flan, first run a knife all around the edges of the mold. Place a deep platter (one that will capture all the caramel) over the mold and quickly invert the mold onto the platter.

CASTILLA Y LÉON

TASTES OF THE CAMINO

CARRIÓN DE LOS CONDES

NATILLAS

Sweet Creamy Custard

Natillas are creamy, sweet custards made with milk and eggs and sprinkled with cinnamon. They are different from flan as they are creamier and do not contain caramel. In addition, the custard is cooked on the stovetop rather than baked in the oven. Sometimes they are topped with a "Maria" cookie, which is a rich, vanilla cookie. While the use of the Maria cookie is optional, the best natillas I have had always had a cookie, and I find the flavor and texture of the cookie to be a really nice complement to the custard. In the United States, these cookies are commonly found in the Latin foods section of a grocery store.

I first had natillas in Carrión de Los Condes. It was a late lunch with a group of my favorite Irish pilgrims. We had started walking out in the dark that day and had taken an alternate route. According to our maps, there would be at least three options along the way to grab a snack. Well, the first two options were closed and the third option only had small snacks. While a welcome sight, they did not really satisfy our hunger. We arrived in Carrión de Los Condes, took quick showers, and headed to lunch. We ended up at a restaurant called El Resbalon and the food was hearty, plentiful, and flavorful. I had never had natillas until then, but when the waiter described the custard and the cookie I just knew what I was having for dessert!

Serves 8

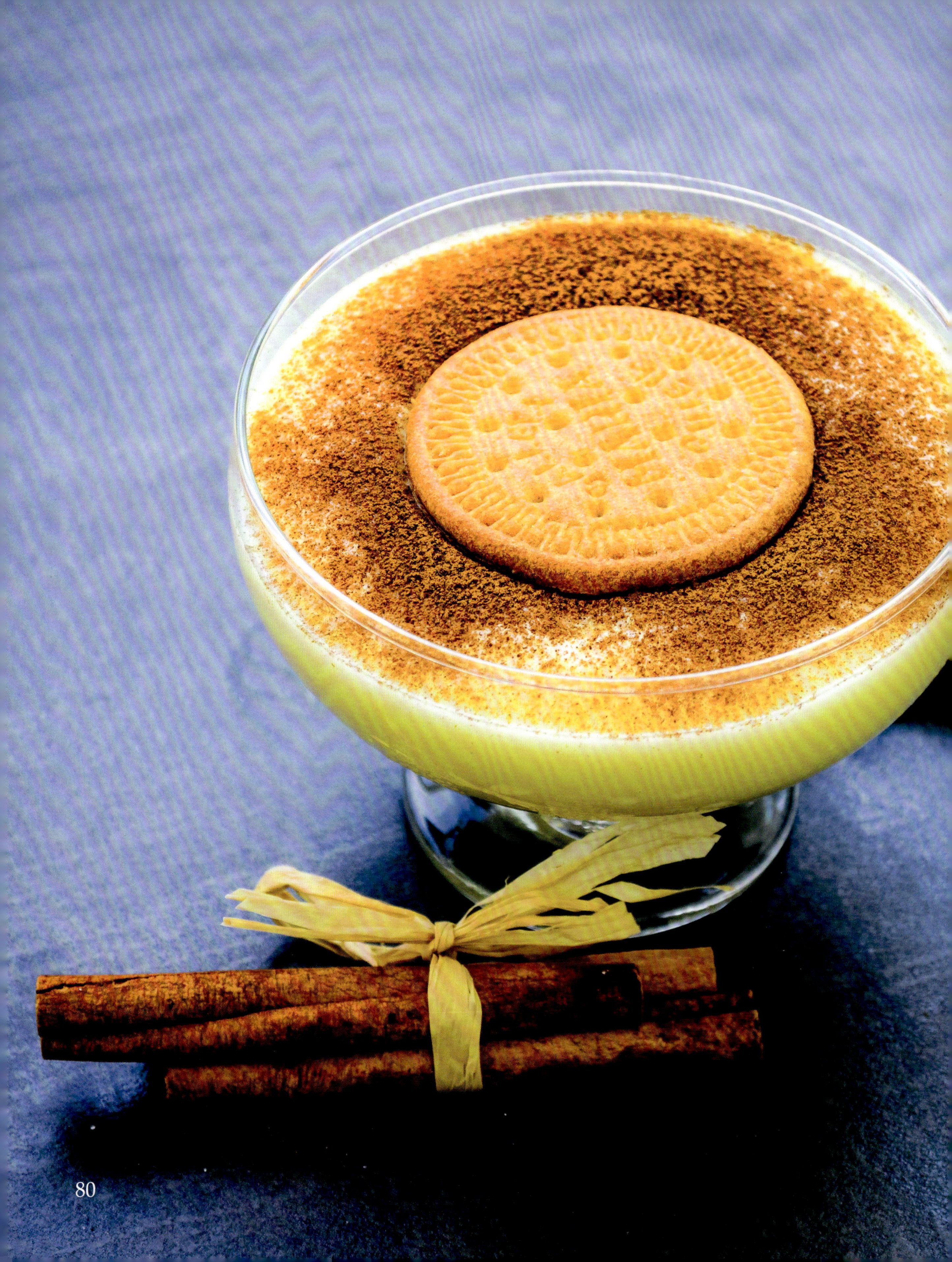

CARRIÓN DE LOS CONDES

CASTILLA Y LÉON

TASTES OF THE CAMINO

NATILLAS

Sweet Creamy Custard

INGREDIENTS

- 2 cups (500 ml) whole milk (using low-fat milk will yield a poor result)
- 2 cups (500 ml) heavy cream
- One strip of orange peel, 2–3 inches (5–7 cm) long
- 1 cinnamon stick
- ¼ teaspoon (2 g) salt
- ¼ cup (30 g) cornstarch
- ¼ cup (60 ml) water
- 1¼ cups (250 g) sugar
- 8 large egg yolks
- 2 teaspoons (10 ml) vanilla extract
- About 8 Maria cookies
- 2 tablespoons (15 g) ground cinnamon for sprinkling

In a large saucepan, combine the milk, cream, orange peel, cinnamon stick, and salt and bring to a simmer.

In a small bowl, dissolve the cornstarch in the water and set aside. In a large bowl, whisk the sugar with the egg yolks until they are pale in color, about 3–4 minutes. Add the dissolved cornstarch to the egg mixture and whisk until totally incorporated.

While whisking the egg mixture, gradually add in half of the milk mixture. Then, once this is combined, pour the egg and milk mixture back into the saucepan. Whisk the custard over medium heat for about 10 minutes, or until very thick. Do not leave the saucepan unattended; because once the custard begins to thicken, it will progress quite quickly. Whisk in the vanilla. Transfer the custard to a large bowl and remove the orange peel and the cinnamon stick. Cover with a piece of plastic wrap pressed directly onto the surface of the custard and refrigerate for at least 2 hours.

After the custard has cooled, ladle the custard into 8 individual ramekins and place a Maria cookie on top of each. It is best to do this about an hour before serving so the cookie has time to soften. Right before serving, sprinkle with ground cinnamon.

CASTILLA Y LÉON

TASTES OF THE CAMINO

LÉON

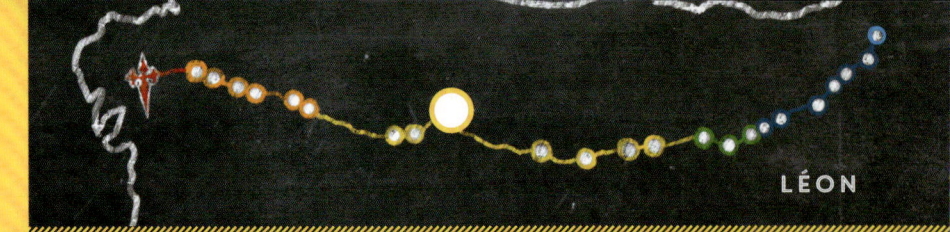

PAN CON TOMATE Y JAMÓN SERRANO

Toasted Bread with Tomato and Serrano Ham

León is a popular place for pilgrims to take a rest day. It is rich in culture and history, has all the services a pilgrim might need, and, at least by pilgrim standards, it has a lively nightlife! Unlike the small towns along the Camino that cater primarily to pilgrims, it is almost impossible to find dinner before nine o'clock in the big cities. If you want a meal before then, your only option is to go to a tapas bar and experiment with all the lovely small appetizer dishes that the Spanish are well known for. In León, a good place to find tapas is the neighborhood known as the Barrio Húmedo. In the following pages, you will find five tapas recipes that are ideal for easy entertaining.

The first recipe is *Pan con Tomate y Jamón Serrano*. Serrano ham is Spain's national treasure, shared by everyone. Cured for at least a year, it has a deep, salty flavor and firm texture. In this tapa, the saltiness of the ham is softened by the freshness of the tomatoes and the fruitiness of the olive oil. Typically, the bread is rubbed with tomato and sometimes garlic and then drizzled with olive oil before being topped with the Serrano ham. I prefer putting the tomatoes, olive oil, and garlic in the food processor to create a paste that I can then brush on to the toasted bread. I find that this produces a much more flavorful tapa.

Makes 18 tapas

84

CASTILLA Y LÉON
TASTES OF THE CAMINO

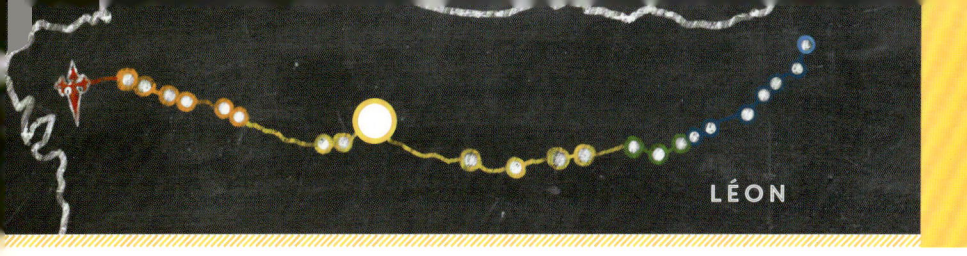

LÉON

PAN CON TOMATE Y JAMÓN SERRANO

Toasted Bread with Tomato and Serrano Ham

INGREDIENTS

- 18 slices country or rustic bread, about ½-inch (1.25 cm) thick
- 4 cloves garlic, peeled
- 1 large ripe tomato, cut into large chunks
- ¼ cup (60 ml) olive oil
- 1 teaspoon (5 g) salt
- 1 teaspoon (5 g) sugar
- ½ teaspoon (3 g) pepper
- 18 slices Serrano ham (if you cannot find Serrano ham in your area, you can substitute prosciutto)

Preheat the oven at 250°F (120°C).

Place the bread slices on a baking sheet and toast in the oven for about 15–20 minutes.

In the meantime, process the garlic cloves in a food processor until they are finely chopped. Add the tomato and process until smooth. Gradually add the olive oil. Season with salt, pepper, and sugar. Remove the bread from the oven and allow to cool down for at least five minutes. Using a pastry brush, spread a thin layer of the tomato mixture on each slice of bread. Top with a slice of Serrano ham and serve.

Make it ahead: The tomato mixture can be made up two days ahead and refrigerated in an airtight container.

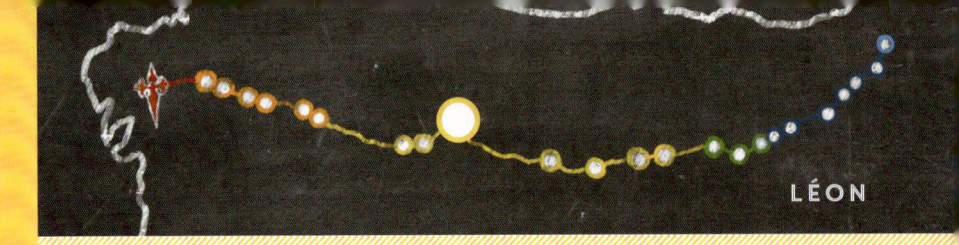

CASTILLA Y LÉON

TASTES OF THE CAMINO

LÉON

MANCHEGO CON MEMBRILLO

Manchego Cheese with Quince Paste

This simple, yet splendid, tapa is created by layering the savory tanginess of Manchego cheese with the sweetness of *membrillo* (quince paste.) Quince is a Mediterranean fruit (whose use has been recorded back to medieval times) that is the European predecessor to the apple. Due to its dry flesh and astringent, tart flavor, it is better consumed as a preserve than raw—as in the case of membrillo. Manchego is a rich, golden, semi-firm sheep's milk cheese with a full, mellow flavor. It originates in the La Mancha region of Spain and is aged for at least 3 months.

Makes 12 tapas

88

CASTILLA Y LÉON

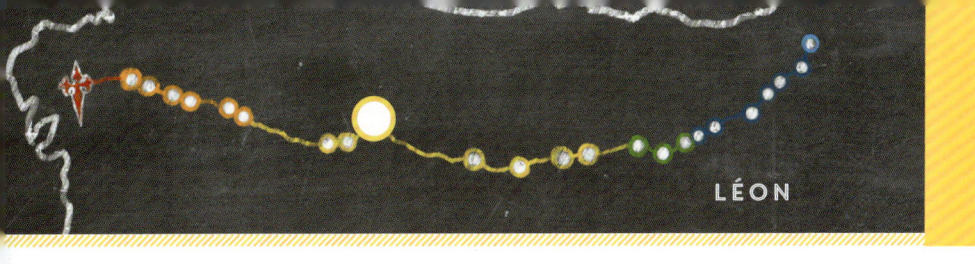

TASTES OF THE CAMINO

LÉON

MANCHEGO CON MEMBRILLO

Manchego Cheese with Quince Paste

INGREDIENTS

- 12 slices rustic bread, about ½-inch (about 1¼ cm) thick
- 12 ¼-inch (about ½ cm) slices quince paste (one 250-gram package)
- 12 slices Manchego cheese

Preheat the oven at 250°F (120°C).

Place the bread slices on a baking sheet and toast in the oven for about 10-15 minutes. Place a slice of quince paste on each slice of bread. Place a slice of Manchego cheese on top of the quince. Arrange on a nice platter and serve at room temperature.

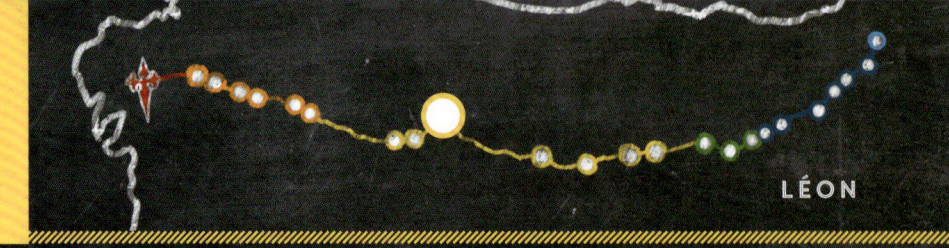

CASTILLA Y LÉON

TASTES OF THE CAMINO

LÉON

ACEITUNAS AL HORNO

Baked Olives

Baking olives with wine, olive oil, and garlic and serving them warm really draws out their richness and aromas. My favorite type of olive for this recipe is *manzanilla*, a green olive with a briny, nutty flavor. However, I will sometimes prepare this recipe with a mixture of three types of olives, which invariably stimulates a conversation among my guests about the different olives. Once the olives are gone, I love dipping some rustic bread into the remaining olive oil mixture!

Serves 8-10

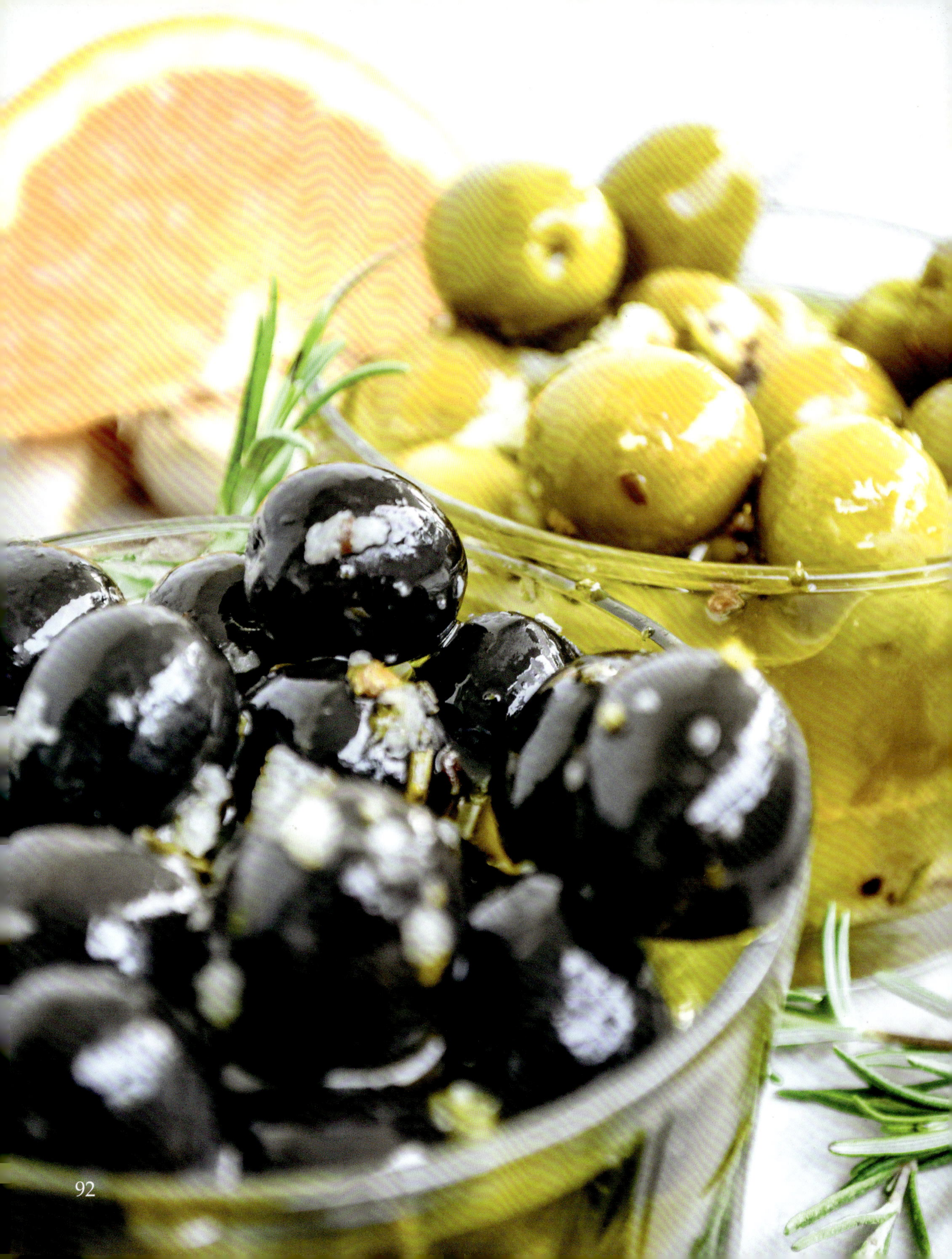

LÉON

CASTILLA Y LÉON

TASTES OF THE CAMINO

ACEITUNAS AL HORNO

Baked Olives

INGREDIENTS

- 36 large, meaty, cured olives
- ¼ cup (60 ml) dry white wine
- ¼ cup (60 ml) Spanish extra virgin olive oil
- 4 garlic cloves, minced
- 1 teaspoon coarsely chopped rosemary (about half a sprig)
- ¼ teaspoon (1 g) dried chili flakes
- Zest of one orange

Preheat oven to 350°F (180°C).

Rinse the olives under cold water and place them in a clay, ceramic, or glass dish large enough to hold all the olives in one layer. Whisk the wine, olive oil, garlic, rosemary, chili flakes, and orange zest in a bowl and then pour the mixture over the olives. Cover the dish with aluminum foil and bake until the olives plump up, about 15–20 minutes. Transfer to a serving dish and serve warm.

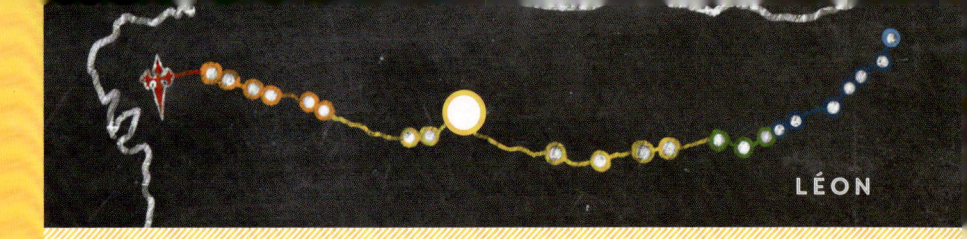

CASTILLA Y LÉON

TASTES OF THE CAMINO

LÉON

ALMENDRAS MARCONA AL ROMERO

Rosemary Marcona Almonds

In Spain, it is common for you to find a spiced or seasoned variety of nuts out on the bar for you to nibble while you are drinking. This is obviously somewhat strategic on the part of the bar owners as the saltiness of the nuts invariably makes patrons thirsty and causes them to order more drinks.

Round, flat *Marcona* almonds are smooth and juicy with an incomparably sweet and delicate taste. This recipe is sweet and savory and herbaceous all at once . . . a truly irresistible combination!

Serves 10-12

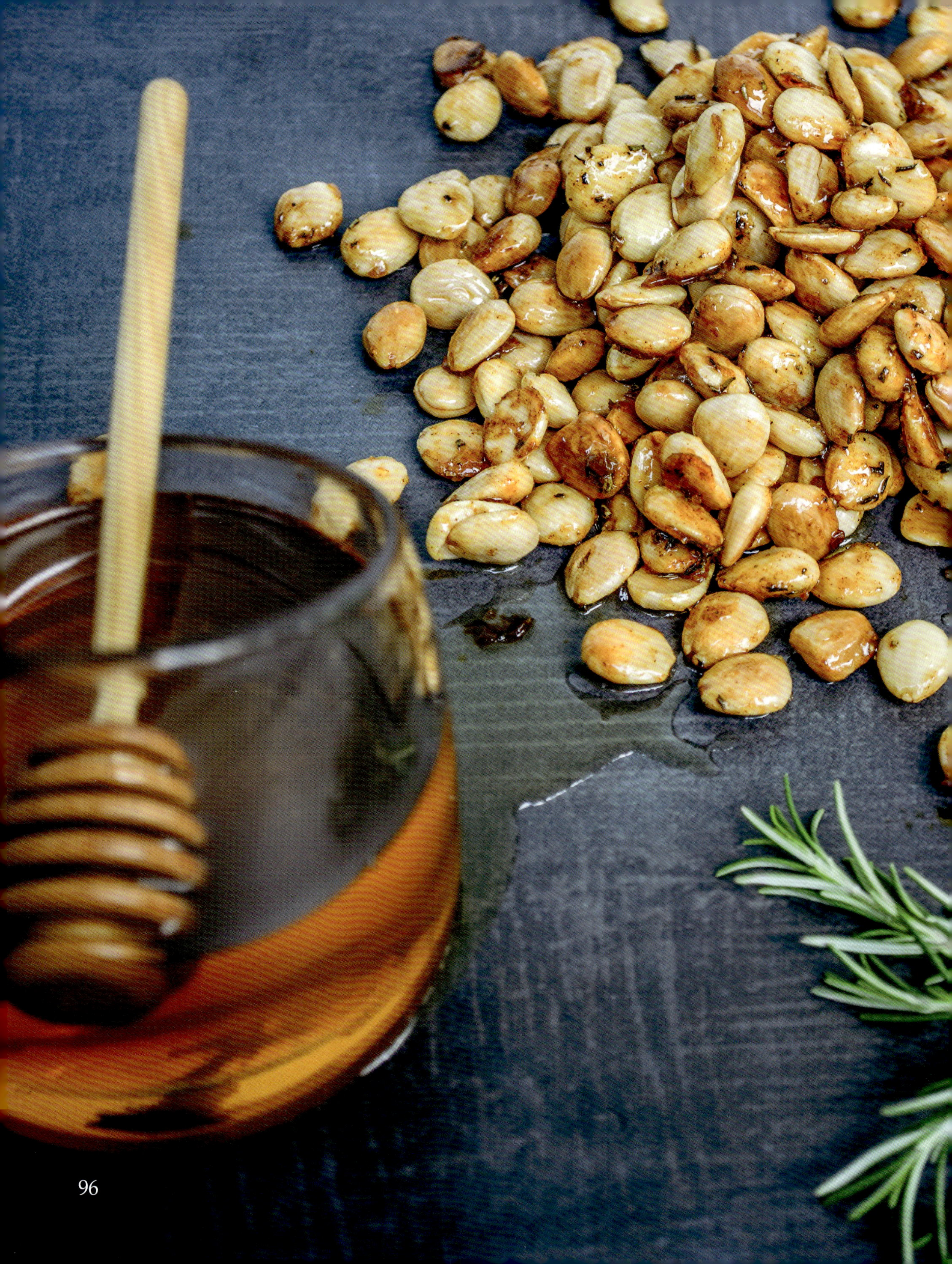

LÉON

CASTILLA Y LÉON

TASTES OF THE CAMINO

ALMENDRAS MARCONA AL ROMERO

Rosemary Marcona Almonds

INGREDIENTS

- 2 tablespoons (30 ml) olive oil
- 1 tablespoon (15 ml) honey
- 1 pound (450 g) blanched (without skins), unseasoned Marcona almonds
- 2 tablespoons (30 g) sugar
- 1 tablespoon finely chopped fresh rosemary leaves (about a sprig and a half)
- 1 teaspoon finely chopped fresh thyme leaves (about 1 sprig)
- 2 teaspoons (10 g) fine sea salt
- 1 teaspoon (3 g) Spanish paprika*

Preheat oven to 325°F (160°C).

In a medium bowl, mix together the olive oil and the honey. Add the almonds and mix them until they are well coated with the olive oil mixture. Set aside.

In a small bowl, mix all the dry ingredients (sugar, rosemary, thyme, salt, and paprika). Add the dry ingredient mixture to the almonds and mix well. Spread onto a parchment-lined baking sheet and toast in the oven until the nuts are a deep golden color, about 15–20 minutes. Stir occasionally while baking. When ready, the nuts should be fragrant, with a crisp coating. Allow to cool slightly before serving.

Note: Once they have become golden brown, the nuts can burn quickly. Therefore, watch them closely. If you can smell them, it's probably too late!

*You can use either mild (*dulce*) or hot (*picante*) Spanish paprika, depending on your guests' flavor preference.

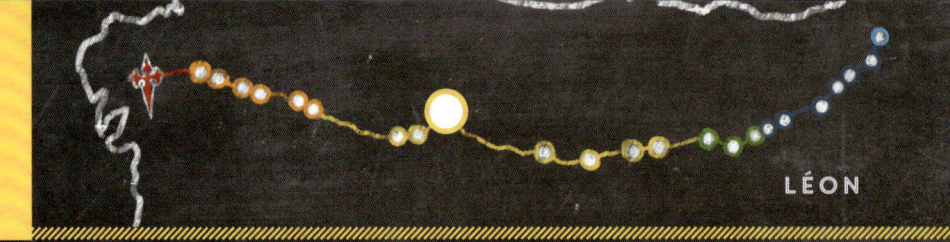

CASTILLA Y LÉON
TASTES OF THE CAMINO

LÉON

MEJILLONES A LA VINAGRETA

Mussels in Vinaigrette

The reason I love this tapa so much is that it is light and refreshing—perfect for summer entertaining! I also love the array of colors and how the mussel shells become the serving dish for the mussels. At the end, I like to scoop any remaining vinaigrette onto some bread.

I typically enjoy these mussels with a light, unoaked white wine, such as an Albariño.

Makes 6–8 tapas

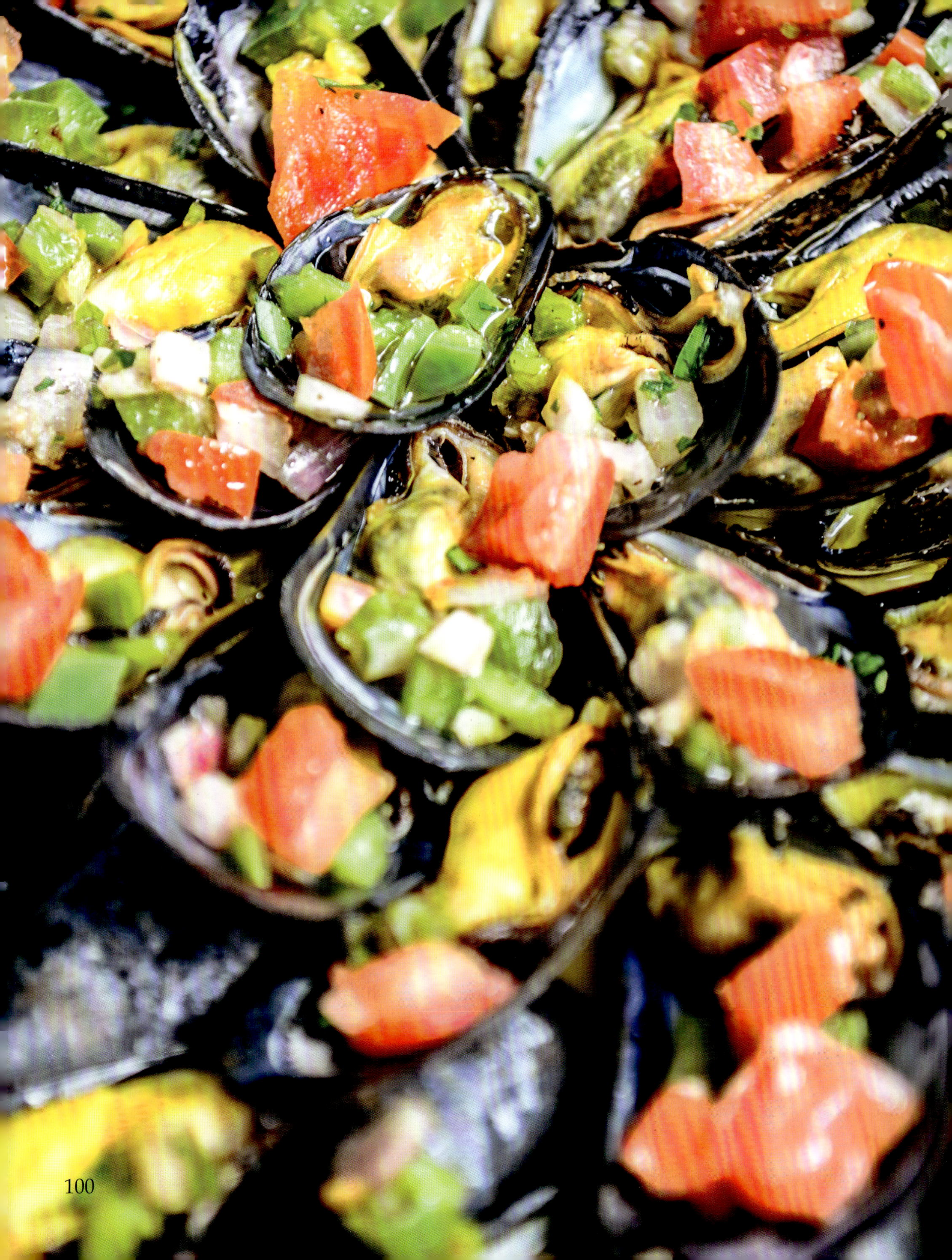

LEÓN

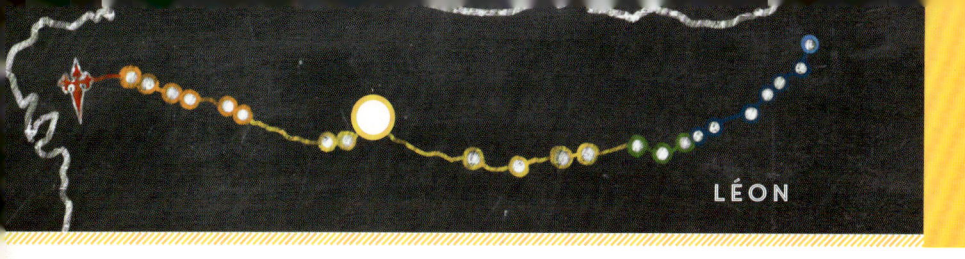

CASTILLA Y LÉON

TASTES OF THE CAMINO

MEJILLONES A LA VINAGRETA

Mussels in Vinaigrette

INGREDIENTS

- ½ cup (125 ml) olive oil
- ¼ cup (60 ml) sherry vinegar
- 2 garlic cloves, pressed
- 2 shallots, finely chopped
- 1 green bell pepper, finely chopped
- 2 medium tomatoes, seeded and finely chopped
- 1 tablespoon finely chopped flat leaf parsley (about 2 sprigs)
- Salt and pepper to taste
- 1 cup (250 ml) water
- ½ cup (125 ml) white wine
- 48 mussels (about 2 lbs, or 1 kg), scrubbed and de-bearded

In a large bowl, whisk the olive oil, vinegar, and garlic. Add the chopped shallot, bell pepper, tomatoes, and parsley. Season the vinaigrette with salt and pepper to taste and set aside.

Discard any mussels that are cracked or are open and won't close up when lightly tapped. Pour the water and the wine into a large pan and bring to a boil. Add the mussels, reduce the heat to medium, cover the pan, and allow the mussels to steam open, about 3–5 minutes.

Remove the mussels from the pan and allow to cool. Discard any mussels that did not open up during the cooking process.

Once the opened mussels have cooled, remove the mussels from the shells and mix them with the vinaigrette. Cover with plastic wrap and put them in the refrigerator overnight. Rinse half of the shells well and store them in a plastic bag or closed container inside the refrigerator. Discard the remaining shells.

Right before serving, arrange the shells on a serving platter. Place a mussel in each shell and spoon some vinaigrette over each one. Serve chilled.

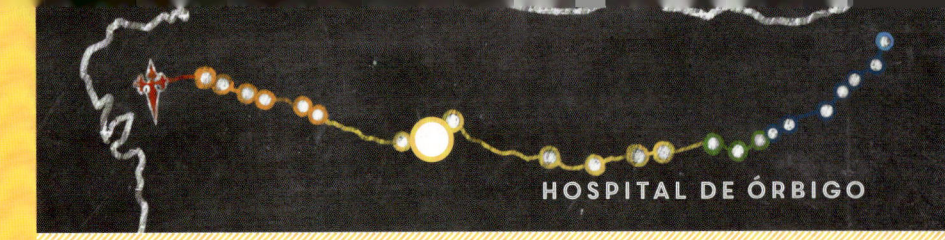

CASTILLA Y LÉON

TASTES OF THE CAMINO

HOSPITAL DE ÓRBIGO

SOPA DE TRUCHAS

Trout Soup

This soup is a specialty throughout the province of León. It is typically prepared and served in a *cazuela*, a Spanish clay bowl or deep dish. I first tasted this soup at Casa Ángeles in Hospital de Órbigo.

Hospital de Órbigo is particularly well known for this dish, as the town sits right in the Órbigo river basin, where a lot of trout can be found. While the main ingredients are simple (bread, garlic, and trout), the seasonings make this soup quite robust.

Serves 4

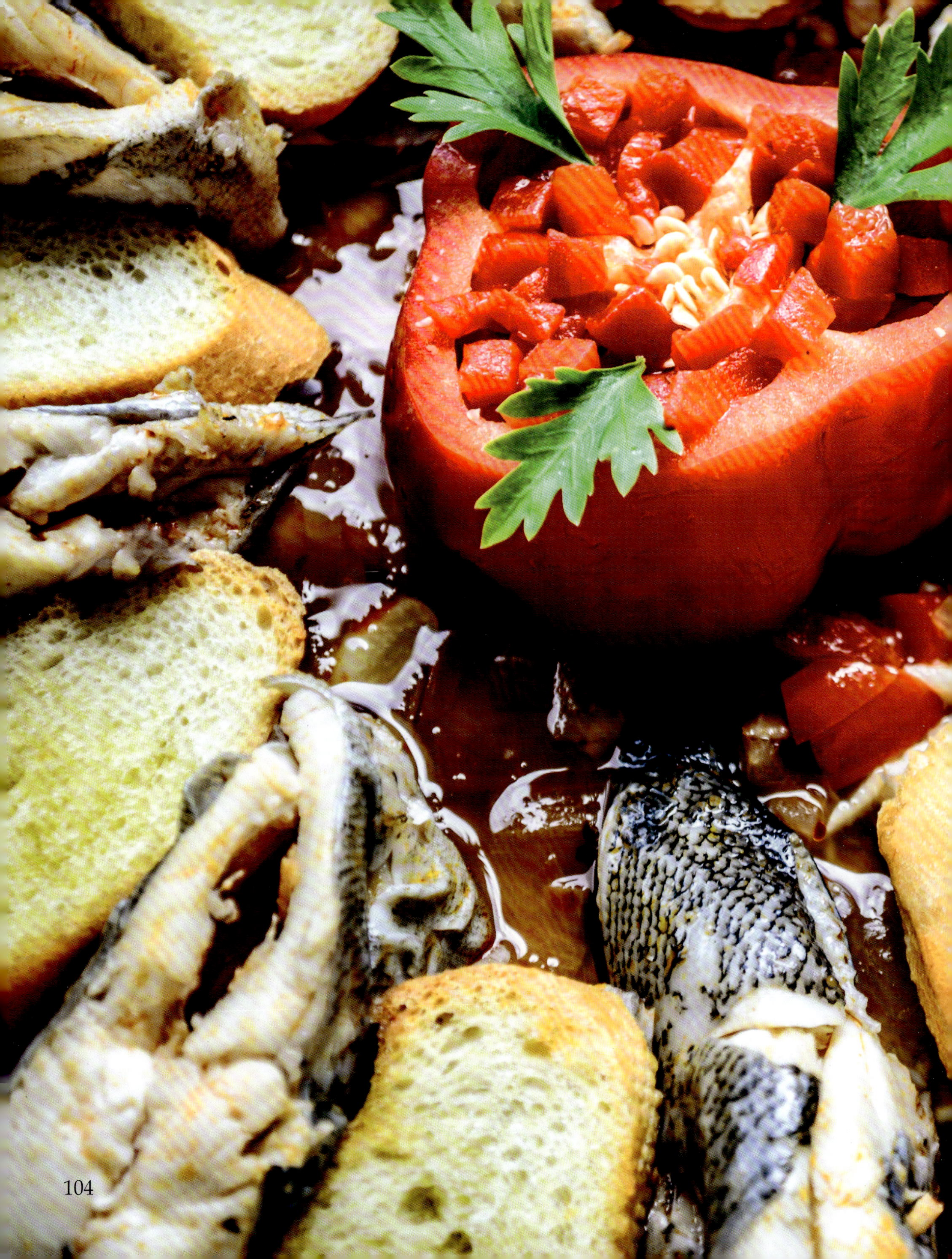

HOSPITAL DE ÓRBIGO

CASTILLA Y LÉON

TASTES OF THE CAMINO

SOPA DE TRUCHAS

Trout Soup

INGREDIENTS

- 2 tablespoons (30 ml) olive oil
- 1 onion, finely chopped
- 1 roasted red bell pepper, chopped
- 4 garlic cloves, finely sliced
- 1 teaspoon (2 g) dried chili flakes
- 1 tablespoon (9 g) mild (dulce) Spanish paprika
- 6 cups (1.5 l) fish or seafood stock
- 2 bay leaves
- 4 rainbow trout, gutted and scaled (about 2 lbs, or 1 kg)
- 4 slices of rustic bread, about 1-inch thick
- 2 tablespoons finely chopped flat leaf parsley (about 4 sprigs)
- Salt and pepper to taste

Heat a large sauté pan and add the olive oil. When the oil is heated, add the onion, bell pepper, garlic, and chili flakes. Sauté until softened, 6–8 minutes. Stir in the paprika and then gradually add the stock while whisking. Add the bay leaves. Bring to a boil and then simmer, uncovered, for about 20 minutes. Season to taste with salt and pepper.

In the meantime, cut each trout crosswise into two fish steaks (each about 2–3 inches (5-8 cm) thick) disposing of the head and the tail. Alternatively, you can ask your fishmonger to cut the trout into fish steaks. Season the trout steaks with salt and pepper. Add to the sauté pan and simmer for five minutes.

Put a slice of bread in the bottom of each cazuela bowl. Ladle the soup into the four bowls. Add two trout steaks to each bowl of soup. Sprinkle with parsley and serve immediately.

CASTILLA Y LÉON

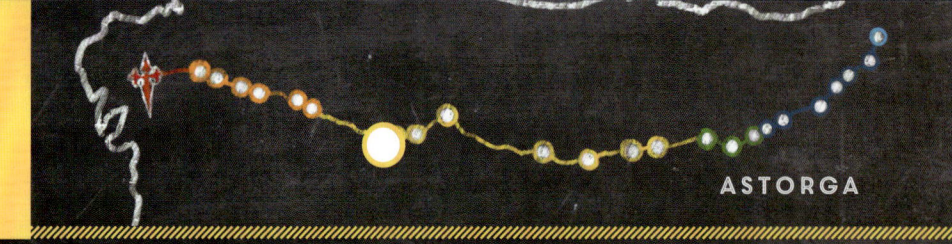

TASTES OF THE CAMINO

ASTORGA

CHURROS CON CHOCOLATE A LA TAZA

Sweet Fritters with Thick Hot Chocolate

The most decadent food experience along the Camino has to be the hot chocolate accompanied by *churros*, warm, crispy sweet fritters. Thick and creamy, the hot chocolate becomes the perfect dipping sauce for the churros. While I enjoyed them a few times along the Camino, one of the most memorable *chocolate a la taza* I had was in a small café in Astorga, across from the Palacio Gaudí—which was no surprise, since Astorga is quite well known for its chocolate.

While the decadence of this sweet indulgence is extreme, it is very easy to replicate at home. In Spain, it is common for people to have a *churrera* (churro maker) at home. This kitchen gadget is basically a large cookie press, and it is available through various online sources, but you can always use a heavy-duty pastry bag fitted with a large star-shaped tip.

Serves 3-4

INGREDIENTS

Churros:
- 1 cup (250 ml) water
- ¾ cup (150 g) sugar, divided
- 1 tablespoon (15 ml) oil (canola or grapeseed, not olive)
- ½ teaspoon (3 g) salt
- ½ teaspoon (3 ml) vanilla
- 1 cup (120 g) all-purpose flour
- 1 teaspoon (5 g) baking powder
- 2 quarts (2 l) oil, for frying
- 1 teaspoon (5 g) cinnamon

Hot Chocolate:
- 1 tablespoon (15 g) cornstarch
- 2 cups (500 ml) whole milk, divided
- 4 ounces (120 g) dark chocolate, chopped
- ¼ cup (50 g) sugar
- ½ teaspoon (3 g) vanilla

ASTORGA

CASTILLA Y LÉON

TASTES OF THE CAMINO

CHURROS CON CHOCOLATE A LA TAZA

Sweet Fritters with Thick Hot Chocolate

In a small saucepan, combine the water, ¼ cup (50 g) sugar, oil, and salt. Bring to a boil over medium heat, then remove from the heat. Add the vanilla.

In a small bowl, mix the flour and the baking powder and add to the boiling sugar water, stirring constantly to prevent lumps, until the mixture forms a ball. Wrap in plastic and set aside at room temperature.

To prepare the hot chocolate, dissolve the cornstarch in ¼ cup (125 ml) of milk. Heat the remaining milk (375 ml) over medium heat and add the chocolate, sugar, and vanilla. Once the chocolate is totally melted, reduce the heat to low. Add the cornstarch-milk mixture and whisk constantly until the chocolate is thickened and smooth. Reserve in a warm place while you finish preparing the churros.

Heat the oil for frying in a deep skillet or pot to 375°F (190°C.) Place the dough in a churro maker (or pastry bag fitted with a large star tip) and pipe 5-inch (12 cm) strips of dough into the hot oil. Fry the churros until golden, turning them once, about 2 minutes per side. Transfer the cooked churros to a plate lined with paper towels to drain.

Mix the remaining ½ cup (100 g) of sugar with the cinnamon. When the churros are just cool enough to handle, roll them in the sugar-cinnamon mixture. Pour the hot chocolate into a large cup and serve with the churros.

CASTILLA Y LÉON

TASTES OF THE CAMINO

VEGA DE VALCARCE

EMPANADA GALLEGA DE ATÚN

Galician Tuna Pie

An *empanada Gallega* is a large, flat, savory closed pie traditionally filled with tuna, stewed tomatoes, and onions. Nutritious, substantial, and easy to transport, they are popular with fishermen and farmers, who take them on their journeys to sea and to the fields. For the same reasons, it has become quintessential pilgrim food for those travelling to Santiago.

I had my favorite empanada Gallega in Vega de Valcarce. Vega de Valcarce is just outside of Galicia and an empanada at the Panaderia Artesanal gave me all the energy I needed to complete the steep climb and cross over into Galicia during the final week of my Camino. Panaderia Artesanal also had other variations, such as chicken and meat, but I'm sticking to the traditional version here.

Makes one 10-inch pie. Serves 8

EMPANADA GALLEGA DE ATÚN

Galician Tuna Pie

INGREDIENTS

Dough:

- 2½ cups (320 g) all-purpose flour
- 1 tablespoon (15 g) baking powder
- 1 tablespoon (9 g) mild (dulce) Spanish paprika
- 1 teaspoon (5 g) salt
- ½ cup (125 ml) water
- ½ cup (125 ml) olive oil
- 1 large egg

Filling:

- 2 tablespoons (30 ml) Spanish olive oil
- 1 medium yellow onion, finely chopped
- 1 green bell pepper, finely chopped
- 1 clove garlic, minced
- 1 cup (250 ml) chopped tomatoes (approximately one 14-ounce can, drained)
- 1 tablespoon (15 g) tomato paste
- 1 tablespoon (9 g) mild (dulce) Spanish paprika
- 1 tablespoon (13 g) sugar
- ¼ cup (25 g) raisins
- 15 ounces (450 g) tuna in oil, drained (three 5-ounce cans)
- 2 hard-boiled eggs, peeled and finely chopped
- Salt and pepper to taste
- 1 large egg, beaten

In a bowl, mix the flour, baking powder, paprika, and salt. In a separate bowl, whisk the water, olive oil, and egg. Gradually add the oil mixture to the flour mixture, stirring just until moist. Turn the dough out onto a lightly floured surface and knead gently until smooth and malleable. Divide the dough in half. Cover with plastic wrap and let rest about 30 minutes.

In the meantime, heat a large skillet over medium heat. Pour the olive oil into the skillet. Add the onion and bell pepper and sauté until

VEGA DE VALCARCE

CASTILLA Y LÉON
TASTES OF THE CAMINO

translucent, about 5–7 minutes. If necessary, reduce the heat to avoid burning the onions. Add the garlic and cook for about a minute. Add the chopped tomatoes, tomato paste, and paprika. Cook over medium heat for about 15 minutes, or until most of the liquid has evaporated. If the mixture is too liquid, it will make the dough soggy. Add the raisins and sugar and season with salt and pepper to taste. Allow the mixture to cool for 10 minutes.

Place the tuna in a large bowl and flake into pieces with a fork. Add the hard-boiled eggs and mix. Add the tomato sauce to the tuna and mix thoroughly. Season with salt and pepper to taste.

Preheat oven to 350°F (180°C).

Flour your rolling surface and roll out half of the dough into a circle about 11 inches (28 cm) in diameter, and about ¼-inch (½-cm) thick, and place onto a parchment-lined baking sheet. Spoon the tuna mixture onto the dough, leaving a one-inch border around the edge. Roll out the second half of the dough to approximately the same size as the first. Cover the filling with the second sheet of dough, pinching the edges together with your thumb or with a fork. Make a tiny hole in the center of the top crust of the empanada so steam can escape during baking.

Brush the empanada with the beaten egg. Bake in the oven for about 40–45 minutes or until golden brown. Allow to rest for at least 10 minutes before serving.

Make it ahead: The filling can be made up to three days ahead. Simply store in an airtight container in the refrigerator.

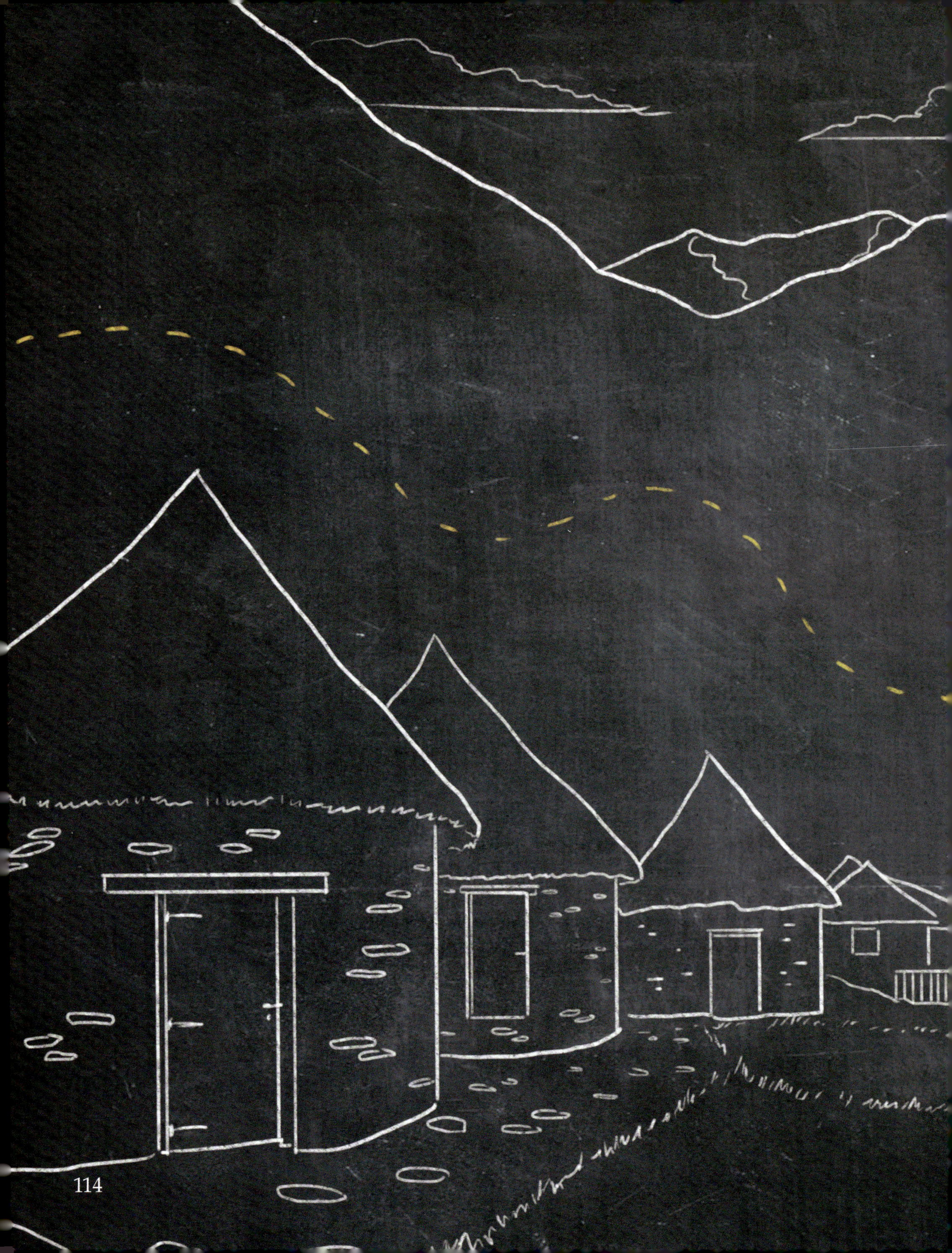

TASTES OF THE CAMINO

GALICIA

GALICIA
TASTES OF THE CAMINO

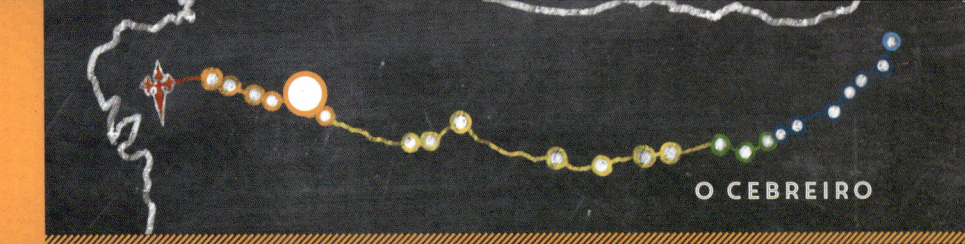

O CEBREIRO

CALDO GALLEGO

Galician White Bean and Greens Soup

While I have enjoyed *Caldo Gallego* all over Galicia on numerous occasions, if I had to choose one city that typifies this white bean and kale/turnip green soup, it would be O Cebreiro. Especially because, after you are done with the long climb up to O Cebreiro, you definitely want something hearty and filling, and I am not sure what could be heartier than this soup. In addition, given that O Cebreiro is one of the coldest areas along the Camino and the evenings can be chilly, Caldo Gallego surely warms up your soul and bones.

The one ingredient that makes any good Caldo Gallego excellent is *unto*. "Unto" is pork fat preserved in salt. It gives the soup its characteristic meaty flavor along with a buttery mouth feel. Unto can be found in Spanish or Latin grocery stores. If you cannot find unto, you can substitute equal amounts of fatback or pork belly.

Serves 6–8

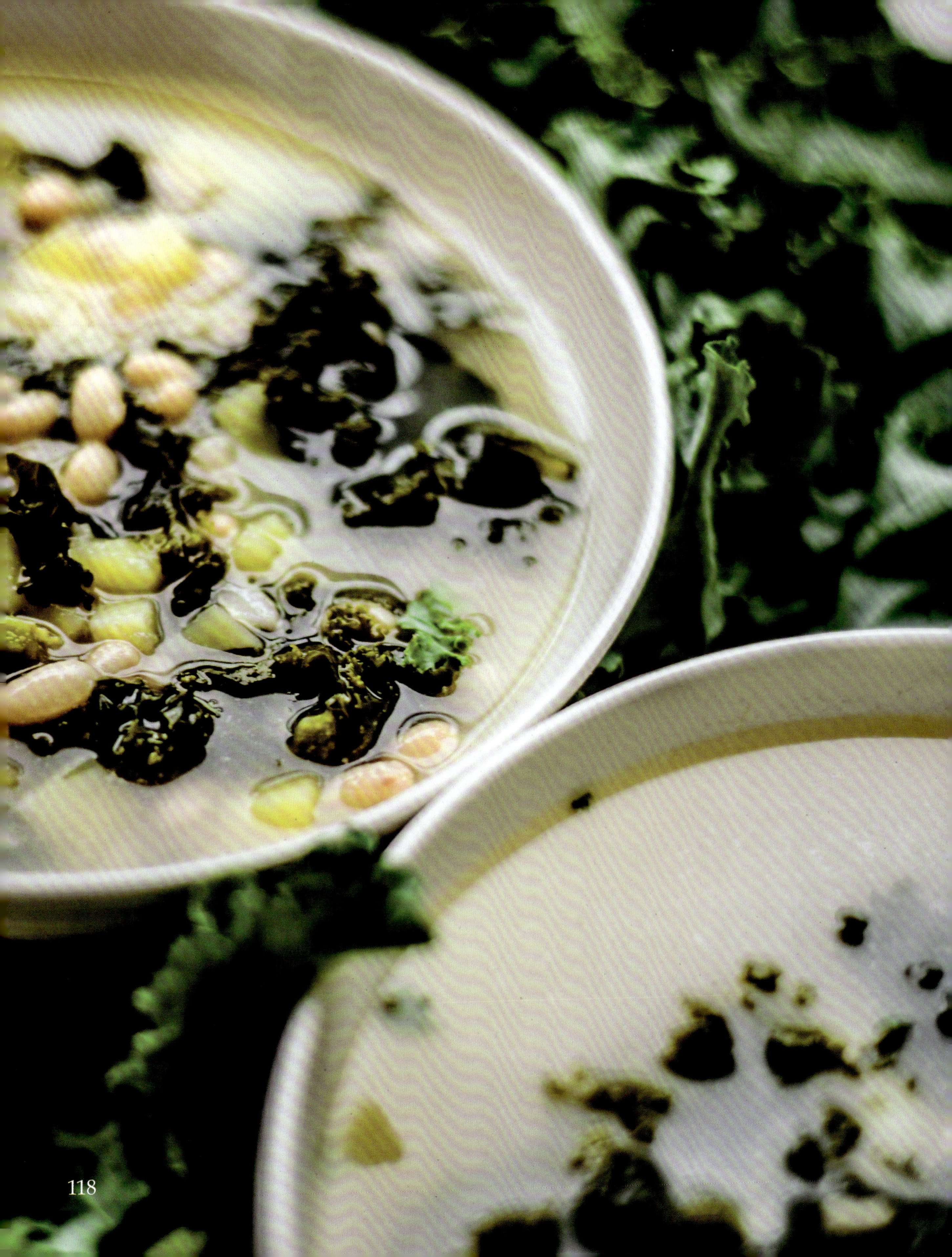

O CEBREIRO

GALICIA

TASTES OF THE CAMINO

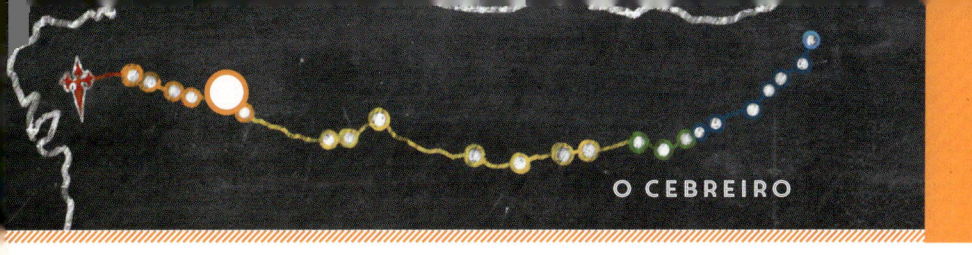

CALDO GALLEGO

Galician White Bean and Greens Soup

INGREDIENTS

- 1½ cups (240 g) white navy beans
- 8 cups (2 l) water
- 2 oz (60 g) unto (no need to rinse the salt off)
- 1 pound (450 g) potatoes, peeled and cut into small cubes (about two medium potatoes)
- ½ pound (225 g) turnip greens or kale (or a combination of both), shredded

Soak the beans overnight in about four cups of water. The next day, drain and rinse the beans, then place them in a large stockpot and add the water and unto (or fatback or pork belly). Bring the water to a boil, then reduce the heat to medium/low. Cover the pot and simmer for about 30–40 minutes, or until the beans become tender. By this point, the unto will have mostly melted away into the stock, leaving behind a tough rind. Remove and discard the rind. Add the potatoes and the turnip greens (or kale). Taste the soup and only season with salt and pepper if necessary. If, on the other hand, it is too salty, add some water to dilute the saltiness.

Cook for another 15-20 minutes or until the potatoes are tender. Serve with some crusty bread.

Note: If your are using fatback or pork belly, you will need to add a bit more salt than if you are using unto, which is already salted.

GALICIA
TASTES OF THE CAMINO

BARBADELO

PAELLA MIXTA

Chicken and Shellfish Paella

Originally from Valencia, *paella* derives its name from the *paellera*, the two-handled wide, shallow container in which it is prepared. It is difficult to find decent paella along the Camino, as many establishments sell a frozen product that does not do justice to Spain's national dish. However, at Casa Barbadelo in the small hamlet of Barbadelo, I had an exquisite homemade paella that reminded me why I enjoy making this dish!

In Spain, most *paellas mixtas* are made with a combination of shellfish and rabbit. As rabbit can be difficult to find in the United States, I often use chicken. Traditionally, paellas are cooked over an open fire, but if you don't have an open fire or paella burner available, I find that cooking it on the grill yields an excellent result and is a lovely way to entertain. Paelleras are sold in many diameters, all usually marked with the appropriate number of servings. This recipe calls for a 13.5 inches/34 cm pan, perfect for serving six. An excellent paella will have a caramelized rice crust, called *socarrat*, in the bottom of the pan when it is done.

Serves 6

PAELLA MIXTA

Chicken and Shellfish Paella

INGREDIENTS

- 7 cups (1.75 l) chicken stock
- Four or five pinches of saffron (about 20–30 threads)
- ¼ cup (60 ml) olive oil
- 6 pieces of chicken (I like using chicken thighs)
- 12 shrimp
- 1 small onion, finely chopped
- 6 garlic cloves, minced
- 1 roasted red bell pepper, peeled, seeded, and chopped coarsely
- 1 cup (250 ml) chopped tomato
- 1 tablespoon (9 g) mild (dulce) Spanish paprika
- 2½ cups (500 g) short grain rice (Valencia, Bomba, or Arborio)
- 1 sprig of rosemary
- 12 mussels
- 12 clams
- 1 cup (130 g) frozen peas
- 1 lemon, cut into six wedges

Place the stock and saffron in a saucepan and bring to a boil. Once the saffron is well dissolved, reduce the temperature to a simmer and reserve for later in the cooking process.

Preheat your grill. Once it is fully hot, you are ready to begin cooking your paella. Season the chicken and shrimp with salt and pepper. Coat the bottom of the paella pan lightly with olive oil. Add the chicken and brown slightly on all sides, about 6 minutes. The chicken does not need to be thoroughly cooked at this point as it will be returned to the pan toward the end of the cooking process. Transfer the chicken to a plate and set aside.

Add the shrimp to the pan and sauté, stirring briskly until pink and

GALICIA
TASTES OF THE CAMINO

BARBADELO

it begins to curl, approximately 2 minutes. As with the chicken, the shrimp does not need to be thoroughly cooked at this point as it will be returned to the pan toward the end of the cooking process. Transfer the shrimp to a plate and set aside.

Add onions to the pan and sauté for 5–6 minutes, until softened. If necessary, add more olive oil to prevent scorching. Mix in the garlic and bell peppers and sauté for about 2 minutes. Add the chopped tomatoes and the paprika and stir for 3 minutes. Season with salt and pepper. This tomato, onion, and bell pepper mixture is called *sofrito*.

Add the rice and mix thoroughly with the sofrito. Pour in the chicken stock, which has been simmering as you've been cooking. Stir the mixture only once to ensure the rice is well distributed. Do not stir further throughout the cooking process. Add the rosemary sprig. At this point, taste the stock and season with salt and pepper if needed. Bring the stock to a boil and return the chicken to the pan, pushing it slightly into the rice, and cook for about 10 minutes. Add the shrimp distributing evenly throughout the pan.

Scatter the mussels, clams, and frozen peas on top and cover with aluminum foil. Cook, covered, until the mussels and clams open, 5–10 minutes. When you hear a crackling noise, you will know that the socarrat (the rice crust) is forming. Remove from the heat and let stand for ten minutes. Taste the rice and add a bit of salt if necessary. Garnish with lemon wedges.

GALICIA
TASTES OF THE CAMINO

PORTOMARÍN

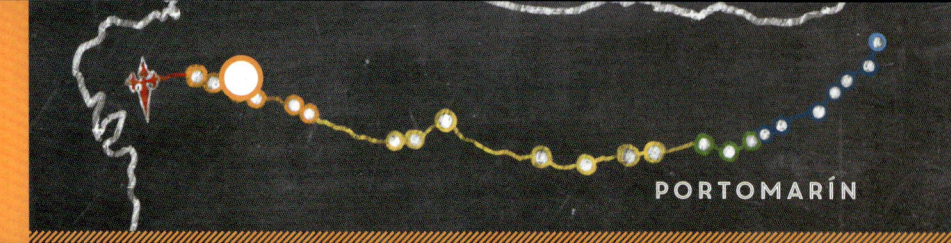

CHIPIRONES A LA PLANCHA

Grilled Squid

On the day that I walked to Portomarín during my first Camino, it was quite warm, despite being early in October. So, while I was quite hungry, I didn't want anything too heavy. Because seafood is prevalent in Galicia, I thought it would be nice to have something from the sea and, indeed, I found a nice restaurant across from the church of San Juan de Portomarín that served grilled squid with a garlic parsley sauce.

The squid can be served alone, with boiled potatoes, or over a bed of fresh greens. Despite its name, this recipe is best prepared on a griddle or skillet, rather than on a true grill.

Serves 4

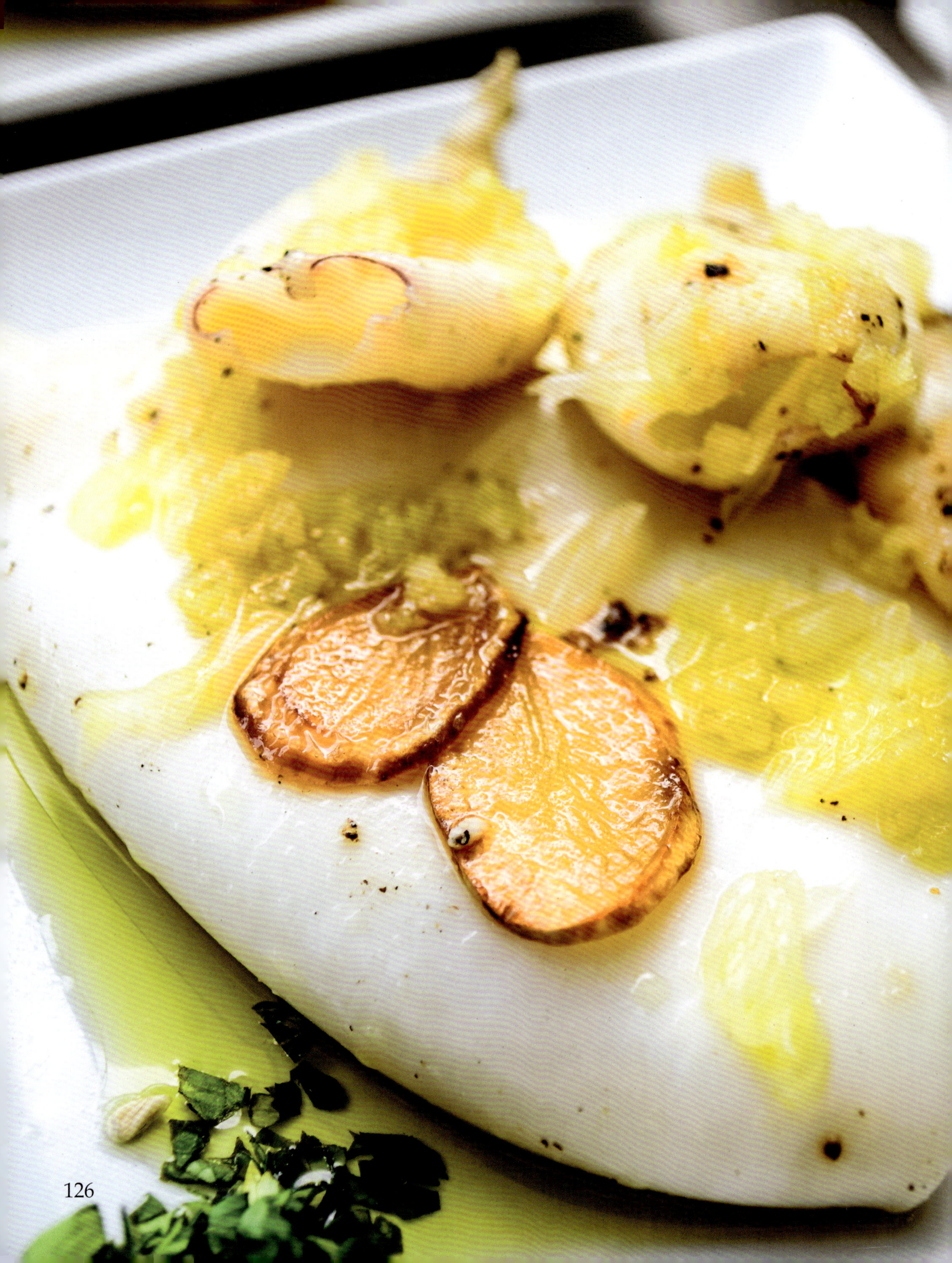

PORTOMARÍN

GALICIA

TASTES OF THE CAMINO

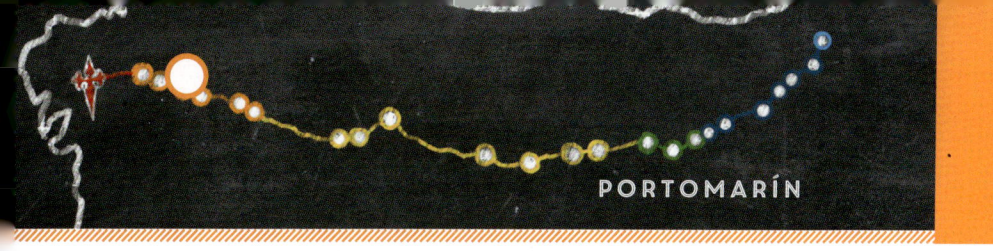

CHIPIRONES A LA PLANCHA

Grilled Squid

INGREDIENTS

- 3 pounds (1.5 kg) squid bodies (about 24, without the heads, arms, and tentacles)
- 2 tablespoons (30 ml) olive oil, plus extra for cooking
- 4 garlic cloves, finely chopped
- 2 tablespoons finely chopped flat leaf parsley (about 4 sprigs)
- 1 lemon, cut into six wedges for garnish

A good fishmonger will prepare and clean the squid for you, removing the innards, the head, and the arms and tentacles, but it is always a good idea to rinse each squid and feel the inside of each body to ensure there is no cartilage left inside. If there is, simply reach in with your fingers and pull the cartilage from the cavity and discard it.

Dry the squid by patting with a paper towel. This is important because otherwise the squid will not brown properly. Score each side of the squid by making a few light parallel cuts on each side of the squid with a small knife—without cutting through the squid. Scoring will help the squid stay flat while cooking, thus creating more browning. Season with salt and pepper.

Heat a griddle or a large skillet and pour in some olive oil. When the oil is hot, place each squid flat on the pan. Allow to cook for about 2–3 minutes on the first side until golden brown, and then turn over and cook for another 2–3 minutes.

While the squid is cooking, place the oil in a separate small skillet over medium heat. Add the garlic and cook for about 2 minutes, stirring constantly. Add the parsley. When the squid are ready, toss them in the olive oil mixture and serve immediately.

GALICIA
TASTES OF THE CAMINO

PALAS DE REI

TORTILLA ESPAÑOLA
Spanish Omelette

While I ate *tortillas* (Spanish omelettes) all along the Camino, I particularly liked one that I had at Pulperia Tera Nosa in Palas de Rei. Unlike most places, where a large tortilla has been prepared earlier and only a slice is served, Pulperia Tera Nosa serves you a whole tortilla, freshly made.

My mother and I obviously were not able to eat the whole tortilla in one sitting, but we sure had a great morning snack. Tortillas can be eaten as a snack, as a tapa (called a *pintxo* in Navarra), or as a light lunch with a mixed salad or gazpacho.

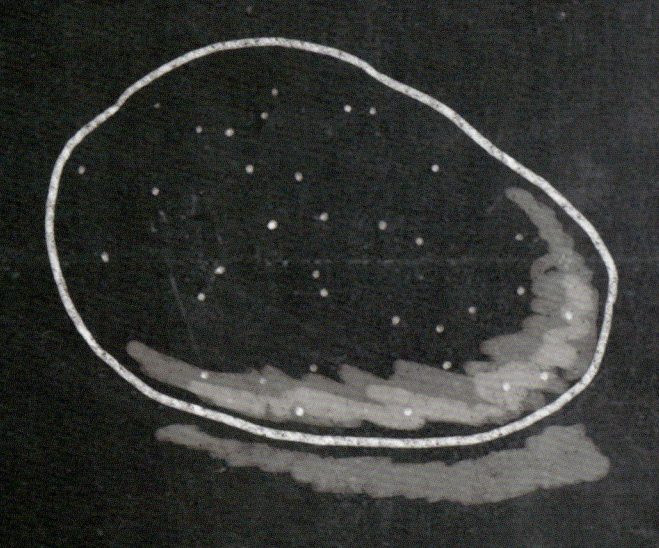

Serves 8 as an appetizer/tapa or 4 as an entree

TORTILLA ESPAÑOLA

Spanish Omelette

INGREDIENTS

- 1½ cup (325 ml) olive oil
- ½ pound potatoes (225 g or about one medium-sized potato), preferably Yukon gold or red potatoes, peeled, and cut in ½-inch dice
- 1 medium onion, finely chopped
- 6 large eggs
- 1 teaspoon (5 g) salt
- ½ teaspoon (3 g) pepper

Mix the potatoes and onions together. Heat the olive oil to medium heat in a medium sauté pan or saucepan. Add the potato mixture to the pan and cook on medium for 20–25 minutes or until the potatoes are tender when pierced with a knife. If the potatoes start burning prior to being ready, reduce the heat to low. Remove the potatoes and onions and drain in a colander set over a bowl. Allow the mixture to cool for 5–10 minutes.

In the meantime, mix the salt and pepper. Beat the eggs and season with one third of the salt mixture. Once the potato mixture has cooled, season it with the remaining salt mixture. Add the potato mixture to the eggs and toss. Add a tablespoon of oil to an 8-inch (20 cm) skillet and heat to high. Pour the egg mixture into the skillet. Allow to cook on high for 1 minute and then lower the temperature to low and cook, covered, for about 10 minutes.

With a spatula, check the edges and the bottom of the tortilla to see if it has browned lightly. Once it has browned, use the spatula to loosen the tortilla from the pan. Place a large plate (at least two inches wider than the skillet) over the skillet and invert the pan. I recommend doing this over the sink as the eggs will not be fully set and may run a bit.

GALICIA
TASTES OF THE CAMINO

PALAS DE REI

Once the tortilla is on the plate, return the skillet to the heat and add one tablespoon of olive oil. Slide the tortilla back into the skillet with the browned side facing upward. Cook for another 5–7 minutes.

Once the tortilla is browned on the second side, slide it onto a platter and wait about 5 minutes before serving—or serve it at room temperature.

TIPS FOR A SUCCESSFUL TORTILLA:

- Use potatoes low in starch, such as Yukon gold or red potatoes. High-starch potatoes such as russets or any potato marked as a "baking potato" tend to be dry and mealy and are not appropriate for tortillas.
- Be very generous with your seasonings, as potatoes and eggs are quite bland by themselves.
- Don't skimp on the olive oil.
- Make the tortilla in two stages: Poach the potatoes and onions in oil and then make the actual tortilla. Most people poach the potatoes and the onions in the same skillet in which they prepare the tortilla. I prefer to use a deeper skillet/sauté pan (or even a small saucepan) to poach the potatoes, and then a skillet for making the tortilla.
  The depth of a sauté pan or small saucepan allows me to move the potatoes occasionally without being concerned that the oil will go over the sides of the skillet.
- About the skillet:
  ◦ It must be nonstick, or else the tortilla will most likely stick to the pan and not come out in one piece.
  ◦ It should be just big enough to allow you to turn the tortilla. If the skillet is too big, you will have trouble turning the tortilla
  ◦ Likewise, it should be lightweight, which will make turning the tortilla easier. By all means, avoid a cast iron skillet. Your wrists will thank you, and you may very well avoid a culinary disaster!

GALICIA
TASTES OF THE CAMINO

MELIDE

PULPO A LA GALLEGA

Galician-style Octopus

Melide, considered Spain's octopus capital, is situated right on the Camino. Whether you are spending the night there or not, you should really consider stopping at one of the various *pulperias* (restaurants specializing in octopus) in town for *pulpo a la gallega* (also known as *pulpo a la feira*.)

While there are many well-known places to eat pulpo in Melide, my favorite pulperia is Pulperia Garnacha on the left-hand side just as you enter Melide's main street from the Camino.

Serves 2

133

INGREDIENTS

- 1 octopus (about 2–3 lbs / 1–1.5 kg), frozen
- 2 bay leaves
- 1 onion, peeled and cut in half
- 1 teaspoon salt
- 1 pound (450 g) potatoes, preferably Yukon gold or red potatoes, peeled
- ¼ cup (60 ml) olive oil
- 1 tablespoon (9 g) mild (*dulce*) Spanish paprika
- 2 teaspoons (10 g) sea salt flakes

GALICIA

TASTES OF THE CAMINO

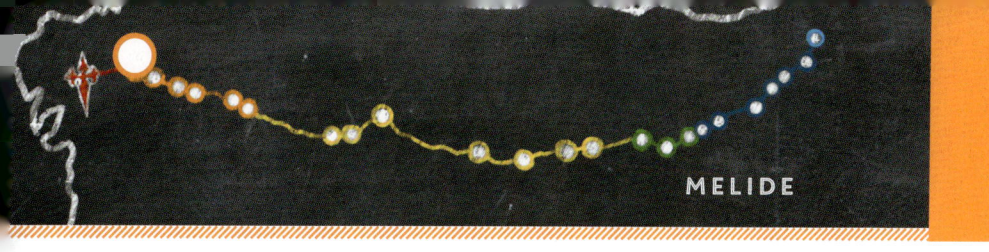

MELIDE

PULPO A LA GALLEGA

Galician-style Octopus

Slowly defrost the octopus by placing it in the refrigerator the night before you plan to prepare it. I usually ask my fishmonger to remove the entrails and the stomach sac from the body of the octopus, as well as the beak at the center of the tentacles. If the fishmonger does not do this, turn the body of the octopus inside out. Pull away and discard the entrails and cut off the stomach sac, which is about the size of a lime. Wash the inside and outside of the octopus well with cold water and turn the body right side out. In the center of the tentacles, you will find a tough center called the "beak." Press the beak outwards and cut it out with the tip of a knife.

Bring a large pot of water to a boil and add the bay leaves and onion. Holding the defrosted octopus by its head, slowly dip the tentacles into the boiling water and remove. Do this slowly a total of three times, then bring the water to a boil again and submerge the entire octopus in the water. Lower the temperature to medium and cook for about 40 minutes. Starting around the 30-minute mark, I like to lift the octopus out of the water every 5 minutes and feel the tentacles to check for doneness. The octopus will be ready when the interior of the tentacles does not feel firmer than the exterior. When it is done, remove the pot from the heat and allow the octopus to stand in the water for another 20 minutes. This will prevent the skin from coming loose.

While the octopus is cooking, in a separate pot, boil some water and add 1 teaspoon of salt and the potatoes. Boil until the potatoes are tender, 15–20 minutes. Drain the potatoes and cut them into ½-inch thick slices. Arrange the potatoes in a serving dish and season with salt.

Drain the octopus and, using scissors, cut the tentacles into ½-inch slices. Place the octopus pieces on top of the potato slices and drizzle generously with olive oil. Right before serving, sprinkle with paprika and sea salt flakes.

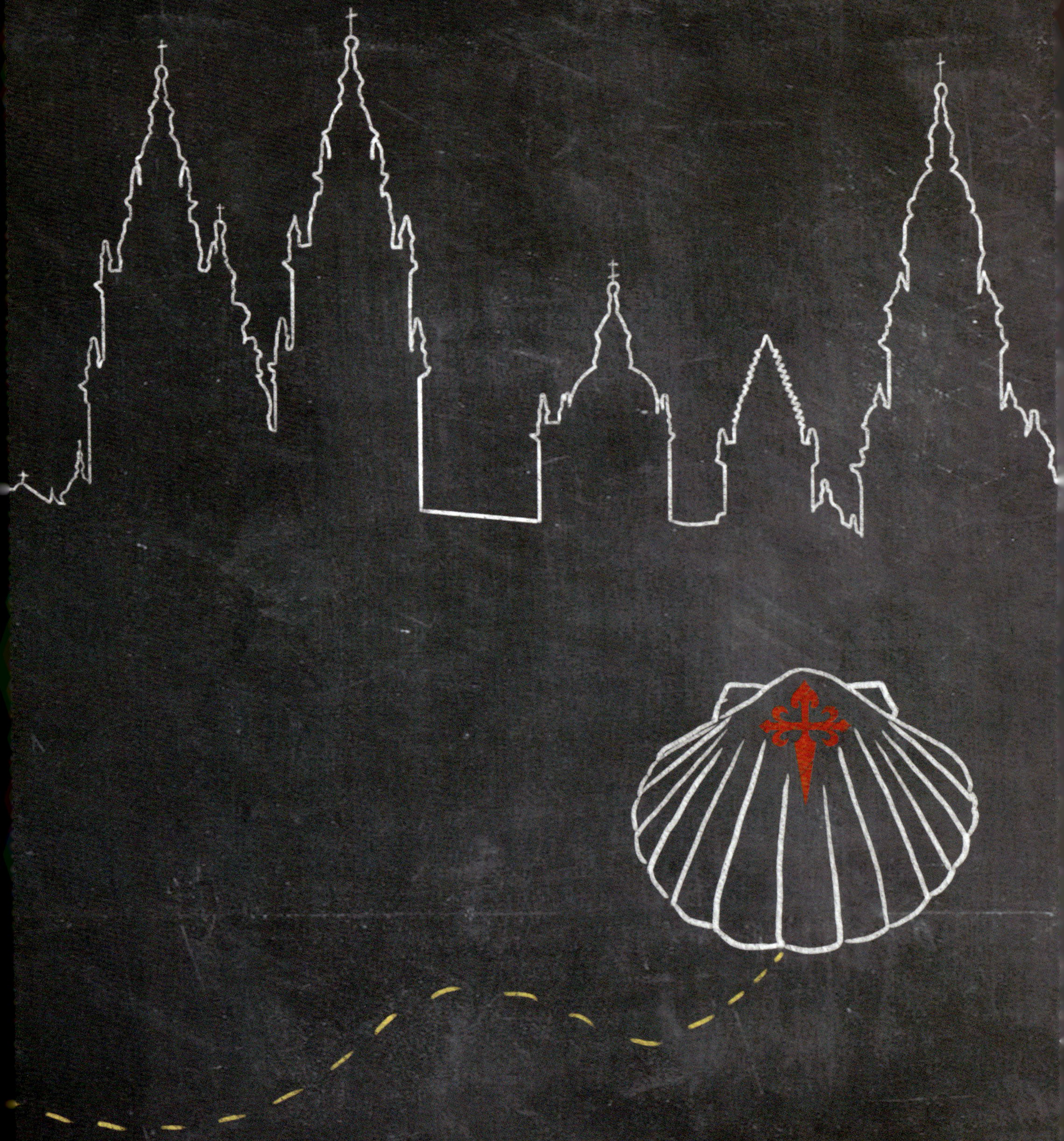

TASTES OF THE CAMINO

SANTIAGO

SANTIAGO
TASTES OF THE CAMINO

TARTA DE SANTIAGO

St. James Cake

This simple, yet delicate, almond cake is originally from Galicia. It derives its name from the fact that it is dusted with powdered sugar using a stencil to create an imprint of the cross of St. James. A perfect accompaniment to *café con leche*, it also makes a lovely dessert for any meal.

I first had the opportunity to try this cake in Portomarín, which is home to one of the largest wholesale bakeries in Spain specializing in *Tarta de Santiago*. While the cakes are mass produced and sold all over the country, when you eat them in Portomarín, you are guaranteed to get the freshest servings. My favorite Tarta de Santiago, however, is the "de la casa" rendition (they also serve a more economical industrial version) served at the restaurant of the Hotel Rúa Villar right across from the old pilgrims' office on Rúa do Villar. I had the opportunity to meet the chef who was working there in 2011 (I believe he has since moved on) and he was kind enough to share with me the proportions of the three main ingredients: eggs, sugar, and almond flour. The remaining ingredients are my additions to ensure that the best flavors come through. When I entertain large groups, I like to "supersize" the recipe—I double the amounts of all the ingredients and use a 10-inch pan.

Serves 8–10

INGREDIENTS

- 4 large eggs
- 1 cup (200 g) sugar
- 1 teaspoon (5 ml) almond extract
- Zest of one lemon, finely grated
- 2 cups (200 g) almond flour
- ½ teaspoon (3 g) salt
- ¼ cup (30 g) powdered sugar for decorating

SANTIAGO
TASTES OF THE CAMINO

TARTA DE SANTIAGO

St. James Cake

Position the rack in the middle of the oven. Preheat the oven to 350°F (180°C).

Line the bottom of an 8-inch (20-cm) cake pan or springform pan with parchment paper and set aside. It is best to use a light-colored baking pan, as the darker pans will cause the bottom and sides of the cake to brown much faster than the top.

In a large bowl, beat the eggs and sugar with a whisk or with an electric mixer at medium speed. Continue beating until the mixture is thick and pale yellow, about 5 minutes by hand or 4 minutes with a mixer. Beat in the almond extract and lemon zest until smooth and uniform.

With a wooden spoon or a rubber spatula stir in the almond flour and salt, and mix gently just until well incorporated. Do not beat the mixture. Pour the batter into the prepared pan, spreading it gently.

Bake for 40–45 minutes or until a toothpick inserted in the middle comes out dry. Set the pan over a wire rack and allow to cool before unmolding.

Unmold the cake onto a serving platter. Using a stencil of the cross of St. James and a small sieve, dust with the powdered sugar. Be careful lifting the stencil as to avoid the sugar on top of the stencil falling on to the cake.

Tip: Metal stencils of the cross of St. James are widely available in housewares stores throughout Spain. While I find the metal stencils very practical, you could however search the Internet for an image of the cross of St. James, then print it and cut out the image to use as your stencil.

SANTIAGO
TASTES OF THE CAMINO

SANTIAGO

QUEIMADA
Galician Flambéed Liqueur

I had a *queimada*, a warm alcoholic beverage of Galician tradition, a few times along the Camino. But it was in Santiago where I got a better understanding of what goes into the *ritual* of the queimada. At the time, I was volunteering at the Pilgrims' Office in Santiago and my good friend John, a long-time resident of the city, hosted a lovely lunch that concluded with a queimada. Queimada is an alcoholic concoction made with *orujo*, a traditional Galician firewater made with the residue of wine production. There are different types of orujo: herbal, coffee, cream, and clear, the latter is also known as *blanco* or *aguardiente*. While the herbal, coffee, and cream orujos are wonderful after-dinner drinks, you definitely want to use the clear orujo for the queimada.

Orujo, a lemon peel, an orange peel, sugar, and coffee beans are placed in a glazed clay pot (can be found in specialty Spanish food stores) and then lit on fire. As the alcohol burns, the flame turns blue and a *Conxuro*—an incantation—is recited. This incantation is a call to the four elements (fire, earth, water, and air) to purify the drink and share it with the souls of family and friends who cannot be present to enjoy the queimada. Once the incantation is done, the fire is put out and the drink is served in small ceramic cups. Traditionally, a queimada is prepared on the night of St. John's day, June 24th. But any occasion where friends and family come together is a fine occasion for a queimada. Personally, I think it is a grand finale for any outdoor evening party as the flame glowing against the darkness of the night is simply magical!

An English translation of the Conxuro follows the recipe. I suggest that you use room temperature orujo, as it will be easier to light than if it is chilled.

Serves 6

INGREDIENTS

- 1 liter room temperature clear orujo (if *orujo* is not available, you can substitute with *grappa* or *aguardiente*), divided
- ¾ cup (150 g) superfine sugar, divided
- Peel of one lemon
- Peel of one orange
- 3–4 tablespoons (15–20 g) whole coffee beans

QUEIMADA

Galician Flambéed Liqueur

In addition to a clay pot, you will need a long-handled ladle and a large lid so you can put the flames out. The ladle should preferably be made out of clay so the handle does not get too hot when you are mixing the flames. If you are using a metal ladle, then I recommend you wrap the handle of the ladle with a tea towel.

Mix ¼ cup of orujo with two tablespoons of sugar in a small cup and set aside.

Pour the remaining orujo and sugar into the clay pot and whisk to combine. Add the lemon and orange rinds, as well as the coffee beans.

Pour the reserved orujo and sugar mixture into the ladle. Light the mixture on fire with a lighter or a candle. When the flame is fully developed, lower the ladle into the clay pot, setting the rest of the orujo on fire. Carefully stir the queimada frequently. If you are bold, raise the ladle to raise the flames, and then pour them back into the pot creating a "fire cascade."

Continue stirring and dipping the ladle to the bottom of the clay pot, raising any sugar that may have sunk to the bottom. Note that the longer you let the flame burn, the more alcohol you will burn and the weaker the queimada will be. If you prefer a strong queimada, extinguish the flames sooner rather than later. I find that letting the flames go on for 5–7 minutes is a good balance between "show" and still having a bit of alcohol left over. At that point, I usually cover the pot with a lid to extinguish the flame.

Pour the queimada into clay or ceramic cups and enjoy! It is to be consumed hot, but be careful not to burn your mouth.

CONXURO

Owls, barn owls, toads, and witches.
Demons, goblins, and devils,
spirits of the misty vales.
Crows, salamanders, and witches,
charms of the folk healer(ess).
Rotten pierced canes,
home of worms and vermin.
Wisps of the Holy Company,
evil eye, black witchcraft,
scent of the dead, thunder, and lightning.
Howl of the dog, omen of death,
maws of the satyr, and foot of the rabbit.
Sinful tongue of the bad woman
married to an old man.
Satan and Beelzebub's Inferno,
fire of the burning corpses,
mutilated bodies of the indecent ones,
farts of the asses of doom,
bellow of the enraged sea.
Useless belly of the unmarried woman,
speech of the cats in heat,
dirty turf of the wicked born goat.
With this bellows I will pump
the flames of this fire
which looks like that from Hell,
and witches will flee,
straddling their brooms,
going to bathe in the beach
of the thick sands.
Hear! Hear the roars
of those that cannot
stop burning in the firewater,
becoming so purified.
And when this beverage
goes down our throats,
we will get free of the evil
of our soul and of any charm.
Forces of air, earth, sea, and fire,
to you I make this call:
if it's true that you have more power
than people,
here and now, make the spirits
of the friends who are outside,
take part with us in this Queimada.

Originally written in Galician by **Mariano Marcos Abalo**

147

INDEX

A
Aceitunas Al Horno (Baked Olives), 90–93
Ajoarriero-Style Salt Cod, 30–33
Akerreta
    Ajoarriero-Style Salt Cod, 30–33
Almendras Marcona Al Romero (Rosemary Marcona Almonds), 94–97
almond flour
    Cream-Filled Almond Cake, 20–23
    St. James Cake, 138–141
almonds
    Rosemary Marcona Almonds, 94–97
appetizers
    Baked Olives, 90–93
    Grilled Squid, 124–127
    Manchego Cheese with Quince Paste, 86–89
    Piquillo Peppers filled with Salt Cod and Spanish Sauce, 56–59
    Rosemary Marcona Almonds, 94–97
    Serrano Ham Croquettes, 60–63
    Toasted Bread with Tomato and Serrano Ham, 82–85
Astorga
    Sweet Fritters with Thick Hot Chocolate, 106–109

B
Bacalao Ajoarriero (Ajoarriero-Style Salt Cod)
    Ajoarriero-Style Salt Cod, 30–33
Baked Olives, 90–93
Barbadelo
    Chicken and Shellfish Paella, 120–123
Basque Chicken, 16–19
beans, navy
    Galician White Bean and Greens Soup, 116–119
beverages
    Galician Flambéed Liqueur, 142–146
    Sweet Fritters with Thick Hot Chocolate, 106–109
breads/breadcrumbs
    Fried Milk, 70–73
    Garlic Soup, 66–69
    Manchego Cheese with Quince Paste, 86–89
    Serrano Ham Croquettes, 60–63
    Toasted Bread with Tomato and Serrano Ham, 82–85
    Trout Soup, 102–105
Broken Eggs with Serrano Ham and Potatoes, 34–37
Burgos
    Fried Milk, 70–73

C
cakes
    Cream-Filled Almond Cake, 20–23
    St. James Cake, 138–141
Caldo Gallego (Galician White Bean and Greens Soup), 116–119

Carrión de Los Condes
    Sweet Creamy Custard, 78–81
Castilla Y León
    Baked Olives, 90–93
    Crème Caramel, 74–77
    Fried Milk, 70–73
    Galician Tuna Pie, 110–113
    Garlic Soup, 66–69
    Manchego Cheese with Quince Paste, 86–89
    Mussels in Vinaigrette, 98–101
    Rosemary Marcona Almonds, 94–97
    Sweet Creamy Custard, 78–81
    Sweet Fritters with Thick Hot Chocolate, 106–109
    Toasted Bread with Tomato and Serrano Ham, 82–85
    Trout Soup, 102–105
Castrojeriz
    Crème Caramel, 74–77
cheese, Manchego
    Manchego Cheese with Quince Paste, 86–89
chicken. see also eggs
    Basque Chicken, 16–19
    Chicken and Shellfish Paella, 120–123
Chicken and Shellfish Paella, 120–123
Chipirones A La Plancha (Grilled Squid), 124–127
chocolate, dark
    Sweet Fritters with Thick Hot Chocolate, 106–109
Churros Con Chocolate A La Taza (Sweet Fritters with Thick Hot Chocolate), 106–109
clams
    Chicken and Shellfish Paella, 120–123
cod
    Ajoarriero-Style Salt Cod, 30–33
    Piquillo Peppers filled with Salt Cod and Spanish Sauce, 56–59
coffee beans
    Galician Flambéed Liqueur, 142–146
Conxuro
    Galician Flambéed Liqueur, 142–146
cream
    Mussels with Piquillo Pepper Sauce, 52–55
    Sweet Creamy Custard, 78–81
Cream-Filled Almond Cake, 20–23
Crème Caramel, 74–77
Croquetas De Jamón Serrano (Serrano Ham Croquettes), 60–63
custards
    Sweet Creamy Custard, 78–81

D
dairy. see cheese; cream; eggs; milk
desserts
    Cream-Filled Almond Cake, 20–23
    Crème Caramel, 74–77

INDEX

Fried Milk, 70–73
Poached Pears in Red Wine, 42–45
St. James Cake, 138–141
Sweet Creamy Custard, 78–81
Sweet Fritters with Thick Hot Chocolate, 106–109

E
eggs
　Broken Eggs with Serrano Ham and Potatoes, 34–37
　Crème Caramel, 74–77
　Fried Milk, 70–73
　Galician Tuna Pie, 110–113
　Garlic Soup, 66–69
　Spanish Omelette, 128–131
　St. James Cake, 138–141
　Sweet Creamy Custard, 78–81
Empanada Gallega De Atún (Galician Tuna Pie), 110–113

F
fish
　Ajoarriero-Style Salt Cod, 30–33
　Galician Tuna Pie, 110–113
　Navarra-Style Trout, 26–29
　Piquillo Peppers filled with Salt Cod and Spanish Sauce, 56–59
　Trout Soup, 102–105
Flan De Leche (Crème Caramel), 74–77
flans
　Crème Caramel, 74–77
flour, almond
　Cream-Filled Almond Cake, 20–23
　St. James Cake, 138–141
Fried Milk, 70–73
fruits. see specific fruits by name

G
Galicia
　Chicken and Shellfish Paella, 120–123
　Galician White Bean and Greens Soup, 116–119
　Galician-style Octopus, 132–135
　Grilled Squid, 124–127
　Spanish Omelette, 128–131
Galician Flambéed Liqueur, 142–146
Galician Tuna Pie, 110–113
Galician White Bean and Greens Soup, 116–119
Galician-style Octopus, 132–135
Gambas Al Ajillo (Garlic Shrimp), 46–49
garlic
　Garlic Shrimp, 46–49
　Garlic Soup, 66–69
Garlic Shrimp, 46–49

Garlic Soup, 66–69
Gâteau Basque (Cream-Filled Almond Cake), 20–23
grains. see rice
Grilled Squid, 124–127

H
ham. *see* pork
honey
　Rosemary Marcona Almonds, 94–97
Hospital de Órbigo
　Trout Soup, 102–105
Huevos Rotos Con Serrano Y Patatas (Broken Eggs with Serrano Ham and Potatoes), 34–37

K
kale
　Galician White Bean and Greens Soup, 116–119
kirsch
　Cream-Filled Almond Cake, 20–23

L
Leche Frita (Fried Milk), 70–73
Lentil Soup, 38–41
lentils
　Lentil Soup, 38–41
León
　Baked Olives, 90–93
　Manchego Cheese with Quince Paste, 86–89
　Mussels in Vinaigrette, 98–101
　Rosemary Marcona Almonds, 94–97
　Toasted Bread with Tomato and Serrano Ham, 82–85
Logroño
　Mussels with Piquillo Pepper Sauce, 52–55
Los Arcos
　Poached Pears in Red Wine, 42–45

M
Manchego Cheese with Quince Paste, 86–89
Manchego Con Membrillo (Manchego Cheese with Quince Paste), 86–89
meats. see chicken; eggs; pork; seafood
Mejillones A La Vinagreta (Mussels in Vinaigrette), 98–101
Melide
　Galician-style Octopus, 132–135
Mellijones Con Salsa De Pimientos De Piquillo (Mussels with Piquillo Pepper Sauce), 52–55
milk
　Cream-Filled Almond Cake, 20–23
　Crème Caramel, 74–77
　Fried Milk, 70–73
　Serrano Ham Croquettes, 60–63
　Sweet Creamy Custard, 78–81

INDEX

Sweet Fritters with Thick Hot Chocolate, 106–109
mussels
    Chicken and Shellfish Paella, 120–123
    Mussels in Vinaigrette, 98–101
    Mussels with Piquillo Pepper Sauce, 52–55
Mussels in Vinaigrette, 98–101
Mussels with Piquillo Pepper Sauce, 52–55

N
Nájera
    Piquillo Peppers filled with Salt Cod and Spanish Sauce, 56–59
Natillas (Sweet Creamy Custard), 78–81
Navarra
    Ajoarriero-Style Salt Cod, 30–33
    Broken Eggs with Serrano Ham and Potatoes, 34–37
    Garlic Shrimp, 46–49
    Lentil Soup, 38–41
    Navarra-Style Trout, 26–29
    Poached Pears in Red Wine, 42–45
Navarra-Style Trout, 26–29
nuts
    Rosemary Marcona Almonds, 94–97

O
O Cebreiro
    Galician White Bean and Greens Soup, 116–119
octopus
    Galician-style Octopus, 132–135
olives
    Baked Olives, 90–93
orujo
    Galician Flambéed Liqueur, 142–146

P
Paella Mixta (Chicken and Shellfish Paella), 120–123
Palas de Rei
    Spanish Omelette, 128–131
Pamplona
    Broken Eggs with Serrano Ham and Potatoes, 34–37
Pan Con Tomate Y Jamón Serrano (Toasted Bread with Tomato and Serrano Ham), 82–85
Pays Basque
    Basque Chicken, 16–19
    Cream-Filled Almond Cake, 20–23
pears
    Poached Pears in Red Wine, 42–45
peas
    Chicken and Shellfish Paella, 120–123
peppers, bell
    Ajoarriero-Style Salt Cod, 30–33
    Basque Chicken, 16–19
    Chicken and Shellfish Paella, 120–123
    Galician Tuna Pie, 110–113
    Mussels in Vinaigrette, 98–101
    Mussels with Piquillo Pepper Sauce, 52–55
    Trout Soup, 102–105
peppers, piquillo
    Broken Eggs with Serrano Ham and Potatoes, 34–37
    Mussels with Piquillo Pepper Sauce, 52–55
    Piquillo Peppers filled with Salt Cod and Spanish Sauce, 56–59
Peras Al Vino Tinto (Poached Pears in Red Wine), 42–45
Pimientos De Piquillo Rellenos De Bacalao Con Salsa Española (Piquillo Peppers filled with Salt Cod and Spanish Sauce), 56–59
Piquillo Peppers filled with Salt Cod and Spanish Sauce, 56–59
Poached Pears in Red Wine, 42–45
pork
    Basque Chicken, 16–19
    Broken Eggs with Serrano Ham and Potatoes, 34–37
    Galician White Bean and Greens Soup, 116–119
    Lentil Soup, 38–41
    Navarra-Style Trout, 26–29
    Serrano Ham Croquettes, 60–63
    Toasted Bread with Tomato and Serrano Ham, 82–85
Portomarín
    Grilled Squid, 124–127
potatoes
    Broken Eggs with Serrano Ham and Potatoes, 34–37
    Galician White Bean and Greens Soup, 116–119
    Galician-style Octopus, 132–135
    Lentil Soup, 38–41
    Spanish Omelette, 128–131
Poulet À La Basque (Basque Chicken), 16–19
poultry. see chicken
Puente La Reina
    Lentil Soup, 38–41
Pulpo A La Gallega (Galician-style Octopus), 132–135

Q
Queimada (Galician Flambéed Liqueur), 142–146
quince paste
    Manchego Cheese with Quince Paste, 86–89

R
raisins
    Galician Tuna Pie, 110–113
rice
    Chicken and Shellfish Paella, 120–123
La Rioja
    Mussels with Piquillo Pepper Sauce, 52–55
    Piquillo Peppers filled with Salt Cod and Spanish Sauce, 56–59

INDEX

Serrano Ham Croquettes, 60–63
Roncesvalles
    Navarra-Style Trout, 26–29
Rosemary Marcona Almonds, 94–97

S
Saint-Jean-Pied-de-Port
    Basque Chicken, 16–19
    Cream-Filled Almond Cake, 20–23
San Juan de Ortega
    Garlic Soup, 66–69
Santiago
    Galician Flambéed Liqueur, 142–146
    St. James Cake, 138–141
Santo Domingo de la Calzada
    Serrano Ham Croquettes, 60–63
seafood
    Ajoarriero-Style Salt Cod, 30–33
    Chicken and Shellfish Paella, 120–123
    Galician Tuna Pie, 110–113
    Galician-style Octopus, 132–135
    Garlic Shrimp, 46–49
    Grilled Squid, 124–127
    Mussels in Vinaigrette, 98–101
    Mussels with Piquillo Pepper Sauce, 52–55
    Navarra-Style Trout, 26–29
    Piquillo Peppers filled with Salt Cod and Spanish Sauce, 56–59
    Trout Soup, 102–105
Serrano ham. see pork
Serrano Ham Croquettes, 60–63
shrimp
    Chicken and Shellfish Paella, 120–123
    Garlic Shrimp, 46–49
snacks. see appetizers
Sopa De Ajo (Garlic Soup), 66–69
Sopa De Lentejas (Lentil Soup), 38–41
Sopa De Truchas (Trout Soup), 102–105
soups
    Galician White Bean and Greens Soup, 116–119
    Garlic Soup, 66–69
    Lentil Soup, 38–41
    Trout Soup, 102–105
Spanish Omelette, 128–131
squid
    Grilled Squid, 124–127
St. James Cake, 138–141
stock, beef
    Garlic Soup, 66–69
    Piquillo Peppers filled with Salt Cod and Spanish Sauce, 56–59
stock, chicken
    Chicken and Shellfish Paella, 120–123
    Lentil Soup, 38–41
stock, seafood
    Mussels with Piquillo Pepper Sauce, 52–55
    Trout Soup, 102–105
Sweet Creamy Custard, 78–81
Sweet Fritters with Thick Hot Chocolate, 106–109

T
Tarta De Santiago (St. James Cake), 138–141
Toasted Bread with Tomato and Serrano Ham, 82–85
tomatoes
    Ajoarriero-Style Salt Cod, 30–33
    Basque Chicken, 16–19
    Chicken and Shellfish Paella, 120–123
    Galician Tuna Pie, 110–113
    Lentil Soup, 38–41
    Mussels in Vinaigrette, 98–101
    Toasted Bread with Tomato and Serrano Ham, 82–85
Tortilla Española (Spanish Omelette), 128–131
trout
    Navarra-Style Trout, 26–29
    Trout Soup, 102–105
Trout Soup, 102–105
Trucha A La Navarra (Navarra-Style Trout), 26–29
turnip greens
    Galician White Bean and Greens Soup, 116–119

U
unto
    Galician White Bean and Greens Soup, 116–119

V
Vega de Valcarce
    Galician Tuna Pie, 110–113
vegetables. *see specific vegetables by name*
Viana
    Garlic Shrimp, 46–49

W
wines, red
    Poached Pears in Red Wine, 42–45
wines, white. see also orujo
    Baked Olives, 90–93
    Basque Chicken, 16–19
    Mussels in Vinaigrette, 98–101
    Mussels with Piquillo Pepper Sauce, 52–55

¡BUEN CAMINO!

WHISK✕SPATULA